Introducing Stained Glass

Edward Johnson

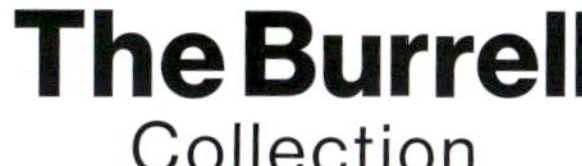

The Burrell
Collection

First published in 2025 by Glasgow Museums Publishing, part of Glasgow Life.
Text © Culture and Sport Glasgow (Museums) 2025.
Images © CSG CIC Glasgow Museums Collection, unless otherwise acknowledged.
ISBN 978-1-908638-49-6

Written by Edward Johnson
Edited by Fiona MacLeod
Designed by Jacqui Duffus
Photography by Enzo Di Cosmo, Jim Dunn, Maureen Kinnear, and Iona Shepherd
Reprographic scanning by Alan Broadfoot and Iona Shepherd
Images supplied by Glasgow Museums Photo Library

https://www.csgimages.org.uk
https://www.glasgowlife.org.uk/museums
https://www.burrellcollection.com

Front cover image: Detail of ornamental panel 45.483
Back cover image: Detail of Tree of Jesse window 45.393.a-c

Acknowledgements

Glasgow Life Museums would like to thank Dr Jasmine Allen, Curator and Director of the Stained Glass Museum, Ely, England, for her insight and support. We also recognize the significant contribution to our knowledge made by the late stained glass conservator and artist Ise (Marie) Stumpff.

We also extend thanks to the many volunteers who help to make the Burrell Collection a fantastic place for everyone to enjoy. Alongside their different skills, their knowledge and affection for the Collection is tangible, and we are grateful to them for their support, past and present.

Printed in Scotland by Mackay and Inglis Limited printers, Glasgow.
Cover printed on Magno Satin Silk 350gsm
Interior spreads printed on Magno Satin Silk 150gsm

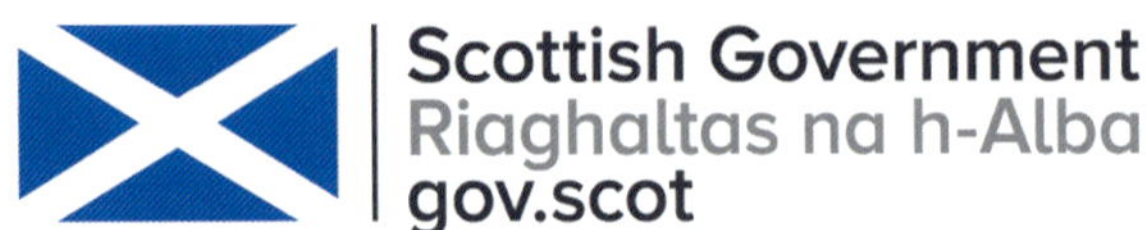

Contents

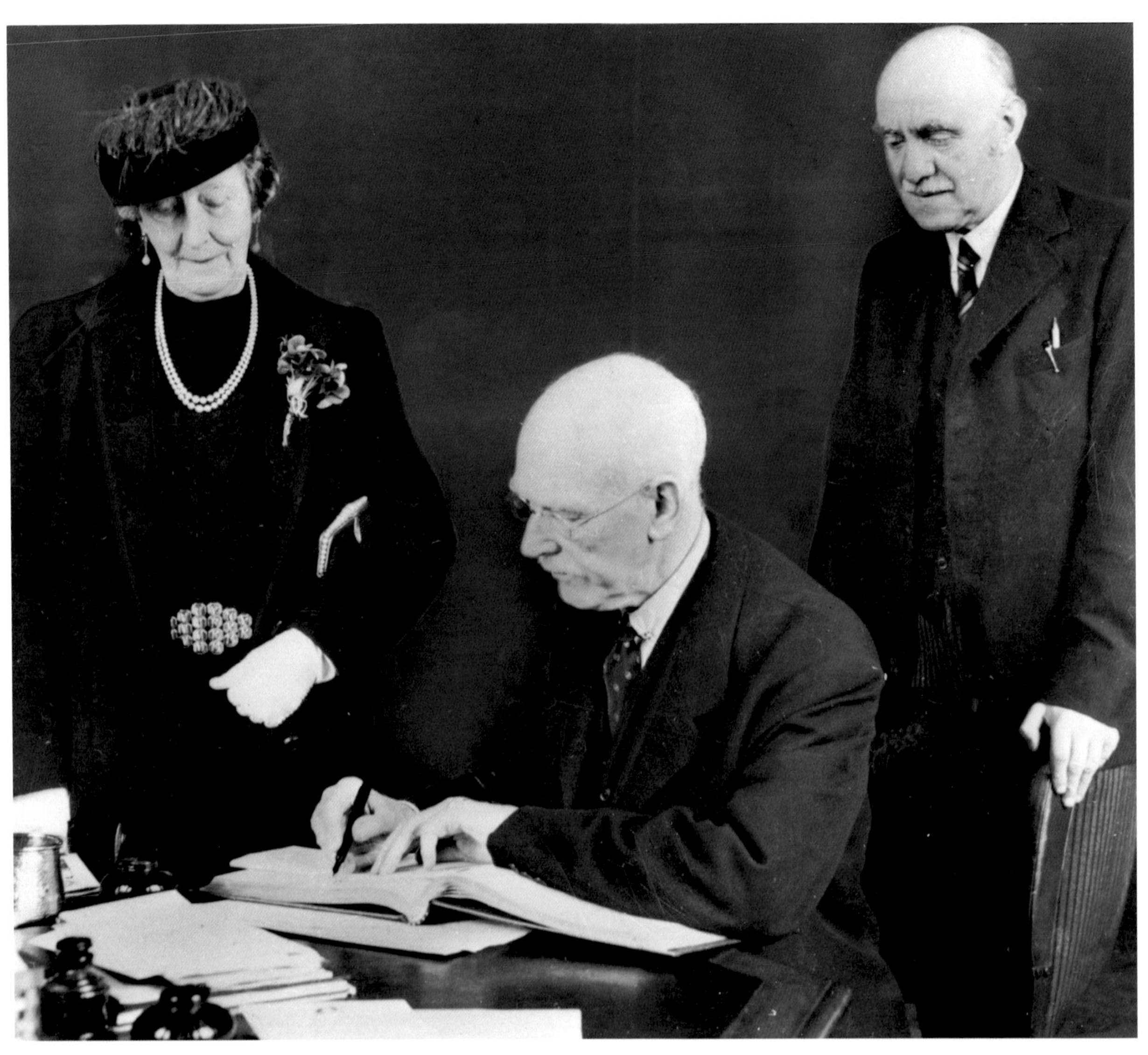

Sir William Burrell (seated), Constance, Lady Burrell and
Lord Provost James Welsh at the City Chambers, Glasgow,
1944, on the occasion of Sir William receiving the Freedom
of the City of Glasgow. © Glasgow Museums Archive,
GMA.2013.1.1.470.

The Burrell Collection: The Gift of Sir William and Constance, Lady Burrell

The Burrell Collection comprises over 9,000 objects gifted to the city of Glasgow by Sir William Burrell (1861–1958) and his wife Constance, Lady Burrell (1875–1961). The main gift, of around 6,000 objects, was in 1944, but Burrell continued to add to it until his death, and the Collection has been further augmented with funds gifted by Burrell and administered by the Burrell Trustees.

Sir William made his fortune in shipping at a time when Glasgow was second city of the Empire. Collecting was a lifelong passion, and his treasures adorned his various homes: archive photographs show tapestries, sculpture, paintings and furniture in his house in Great Western Terrace, Glasgow. These, and also ceramics, stained glass, arms and armour and textiles, were displayed at Hutton Castle, his home in the Scottish Borders.

A sophisticated collector with a discerning eye, Burrell appreciated fine craftsmanship and meticulous attention to detail. From tapestries to sculpture, nineteenth-century French art to Chinese bronzes, medieval stained glass to Islamic carpets, the breadth and quality of his collection demonstrate his wide-ranging embrace of different cultures and art forms. Sir William also gave money for a new building to house his collection, and it is now displayed in a purpose-built museum in the centre of Pollok Country Park, on the south side of Glasgow. The park was gifted to the city in 1967 by Mrs Anne Maxwell Macdonald (1906–2011), and a competition, sponsored by the Royal Institute of British Architects, was held to design a suitable building within it to house the Collection. The winners of the competition, architects Barry Gasson, John Meunier and Brit Andresen, came up with a building which not only displays the Collection to advantage, but is also in harmony with the surrounding parkland. The building opened in 1983, but through the decades the Scottish weather took its toll and in 2016 the Category-A listed building closed for an ambitious programme of refurbishment, redisplay and reinterpretation. The Burrell Collection reopened to the public in 2022.

This series is designed to introduce different parts of the Collection. Written by subject specialists, each book gives an insight into the Burrell's treasures. We, the Trustees of The Burrell Collection, are delighted to see the amount of new research that has been carried out on the objects in the collection, and hope that visitors will continue to enjoy Sir William and Constance, Lady Burrell's gift for many generations to come.

Professor Frances Fowle
Senior Trustee, Sir William Burrell's Trust

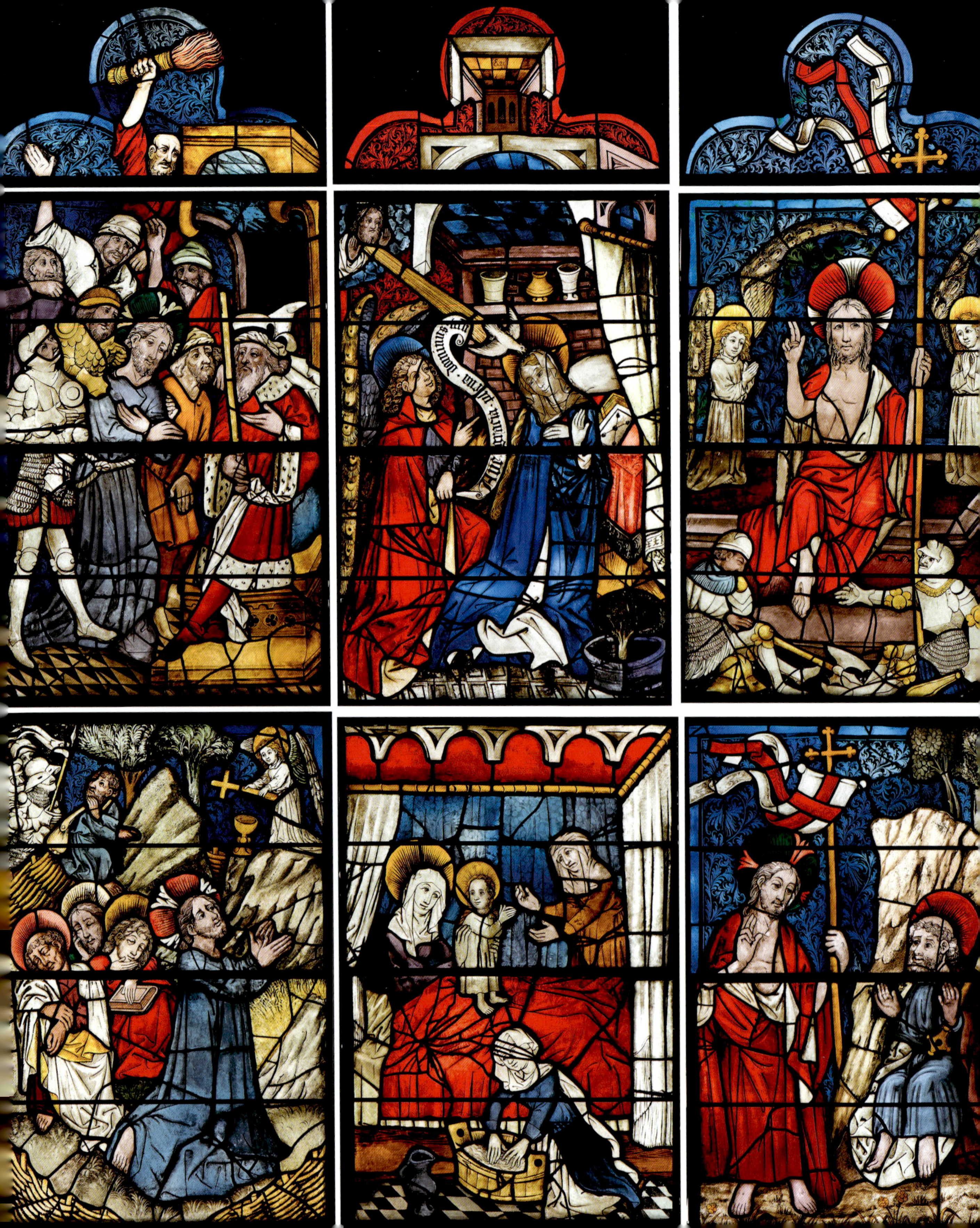

Introduction

In 1951, at the age of 89, Sir William Burrell wrote to the first Keeper of the Burrell Collection, Andrew Hannah (1907–78), and remarked 'our collection of stained glass is large and stained glass, to my mind, is one of the most beautiful of all the arts'. Burrell's admiration for stained glass is strikingly revealed in the outstanding collection he donated to his native city. Sir William acquired approximately 800 pieces of stained glass over the course of at least six decades, establishing a collection that ranks amongst the largest and finest in the world.

Historical stained glass formed some of Burrell's earliest collecting, as evidenced by the loans he made to the Glasgow International Exhibition of 1901 and by photographs published in 1904 of his home, 8 Great Western Terrace in Glasgow's West End. However, it was with the purchase of Hutton Castle, Berwickshire, in 1916, that Burrell began assembling a truly world-class collection of medieval and Renaissance glass which he used to adorn his fashionable Gothic interiors.

From the late 1930s, following his decision to donate his treasures to public ownership, Burrell, aided by his trusted stained glass dealer, restorer and advisor Wilfred Drake (1879–1948), continued to develop and expand his collection.

Burrell acquired stained glass well into his 90s, purchasing beyond his domestic needs and building an ambitious and comprehensive museum collection.

Despite this shift in his collecting practices, Burrell was keen that the stained glass collection should continue to represent his own interests, stating that 'I don't like to buy anything unless it appeals to me'. Subsequently, the Collection is notably rich in fifteenth- and sixteenth-century glass, reflecting his wider passion for the art of late medieval and early Renaissance northern Europe. Burrell did however make significant purchases outside of these parameters, acquiring internationally important pieces of both earlier and later date.

A vast and diverse collection of outstanding quality, Burrell's stained glass collection beautifully represents over 500 years of technical innovation and artistic development in the medium, illustrating changing fashions, variations of iconography, and shifting systems of patronage and ownership across northern Europe. From the monumental windows that brought divine illumination, awe-inspiring colour, and instructive religious imagery to ecclesiastical interiors, to the smaller roundels and heraldic panels that adorned secular spaces as proud assertions of status and taste, the Burrell Collection eloquently showcases the exquisite skill and artistry of the glazier's craft from the twelfth to the seventeenth century.

Opposite: Too large to have been considered for Hutton Castle, these windows from Boppard-am-Rhein were purchased specifically for a future museum collection. Many of Burrell's later acquisitions were kept in storage or sent directly to Glasgow, rarely being viewed by Burrell himself. (Detail of 45.485, see p.40)

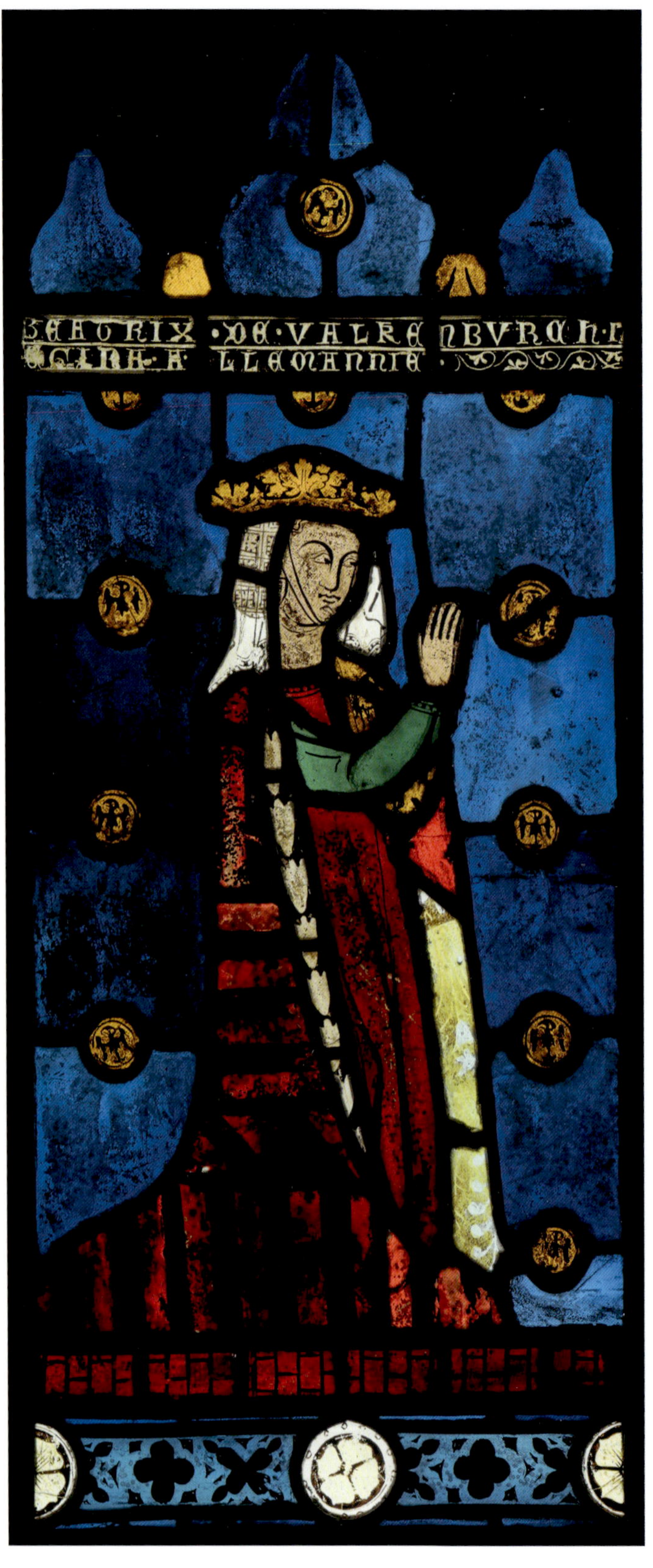

BEATRIX · DE · VALKENBVRCH
...INA · A LLEMANNIE ·

Twelfth- to Thirteenth-century Glass

Although evidence indicates the use of coloured window glass in the Ancient Roman world, it was not until the medieval period that stained glass emerged as one of the pre-eminent forms of decorative art. Associated with the rise of Gothic architecture and the golden age of cathedral building, from the mid-1100s stained glass workshops, most notably in France, Germany, and England, flourished in response to the growing demands of the Church. Influenced by well-established theological concepts of light and colour and their mystical associations with the divine, the Church embraced the opportunities presented by new building techniques to incorporate larger windows and more glazing into its structures, flooding their vast interiors with shimmering heavenly light.

The workshop practices of the twelfth century would have been largely familiar to stained glass artists throughout the Middle Ages. Once a design was agreed upon by the glazier and their client, a full-scale line drawing (or 'cartoon') of the window was typically drawn onto a whitewashed tabletop. In accordance with the cartoon, glass was selected and roughly cracked to size with a red-hot iron, before its shape was refined with a nibbling tool called a 'grozing iron'. Once cut and shaped, the glass was re-assembled on the table, ready to be painted.

Twelfth- and thirteenth-century painted glass is characterized by its simple modelling and strong lines, with details including hair, faces, drapery, and ornamental motifs applied to the surface in bold, dark, vitreous paints. Consisting of ground glass, metal oxides, and a binder such as wine or urine, these paints were deftly applied with a variety of animal-hair brushes. They could be diluted to provide a matte wash, adding shadow and depth. Prior to firing, areas of paint were sometimes removed; dabbed or scratched from the surface with brushes, sticks, needles, or even fingers, to create highlights and control the passage of light. Intended to be 'read' and understood from a distance, a window's design was further defined and reinforced by the considered placement of the imposing lead strips (or 'calmes'), that held the mosaic-like arrangement of glass together.

Survivals from the first half of the twelfth century are rare, with much of the glass that exists taking the form of single full-size figures, as seen in the Ancestors of Christ windows at Canterbury Cathedral, recently dated to 1130–60. However the rich potential for glass as a vehicle for storytelling was soon recognized, and by the thirteenth century windows composed of stacked medallions executed with engaging and dramatic vignettes of biblical stories and saints' lives were a popular means of exploring sacred narrative.

By the end of the 1200s non-figurative, decorative panels of clear *grisailles* glass became increasingly fashionable, with its use becoming more pronounced in the following centuries.

Opposite: Possibly associated with royal patronage, this fine portrait of Beatrix of Valkenburg is masterfully worked. The artist cleverly used both sides of the glass, painting Beatrix's hairnet on the reverse. This gives the impression of delicate translucency to the veil above. (Detail of 45.2, see p.16)

Prophet Jeremiah, about 1144–45
Made in France
Colourless glass, pot metal glass, vitreous paint, lead
63.2 cm x 35 cm x 1 cm
From the 'Infancy of Christ', Abbey Church of
Saint-Denis, Île-de-France, France
45.364

Depicting the Old Testament prophet Jeremiah, this panel originally formed part of the 'Infancy of Christ' window commissioned for the choir of the abbey church of Saint-Denis, near Paris.

Saint-Denis was renovated and re-consecrated in 1144 under the guidance of the renowned Abbot Suger (about 1081–1151), and it was there that the latest building techniques and ideas coalesced – marking what is often regarded as the beginning of the Gothic style. Suger particularly delighted in the abbey's innovative use of light and stained glass, writing enthusiastically on the 'most radiant windows', and their 'marvellous execution', splendour, and expense.

Despite being a target for French revolutionary violence, much of Saint-Denis's stained glass survived the destruction of the 1790s and remained in situ until 1799, when it was removed and rehoused in the Musée des Monuments français, Paris. Some panels were returned to Saint-Denis around 1817–18, and thereafter in the mid-nineteenth century the windows were subject to extensive and heavy-handed restoration overseen by the celebrated French architect Eugène Viollet-le-Duc (1814–79).

Omitted from Viollet-le-Duc's reconstruction, the Jeremiah panel is a rare surviving example of the twelfth-century glazier's art and is the oldest stained glass in the collection.

Acquired in 1923, it was not until 1961, three years after Burrell's death, when stained glass scholar Professor Hans Wentzel (1913–75) identified this panel's illustrious origins.

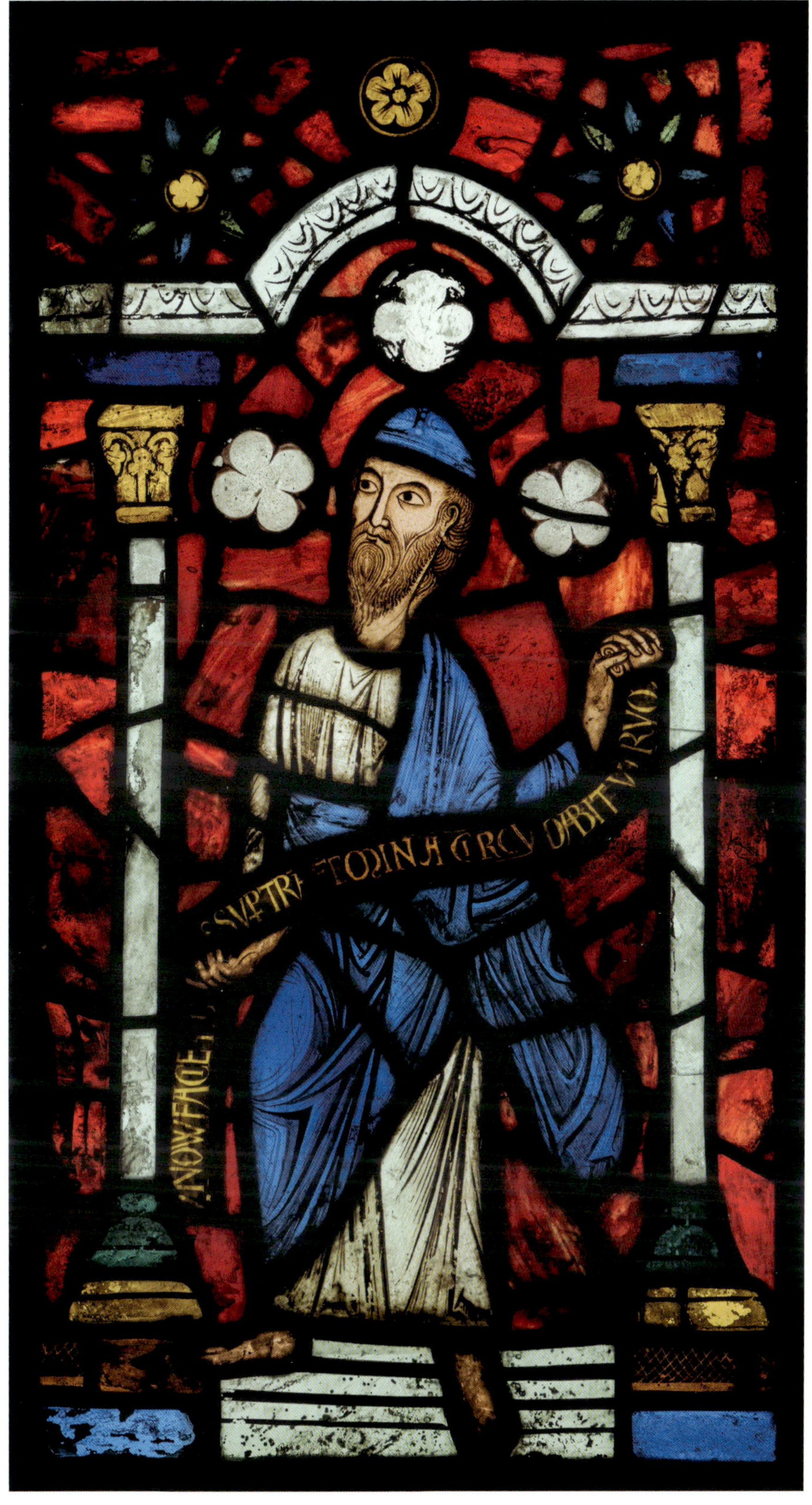

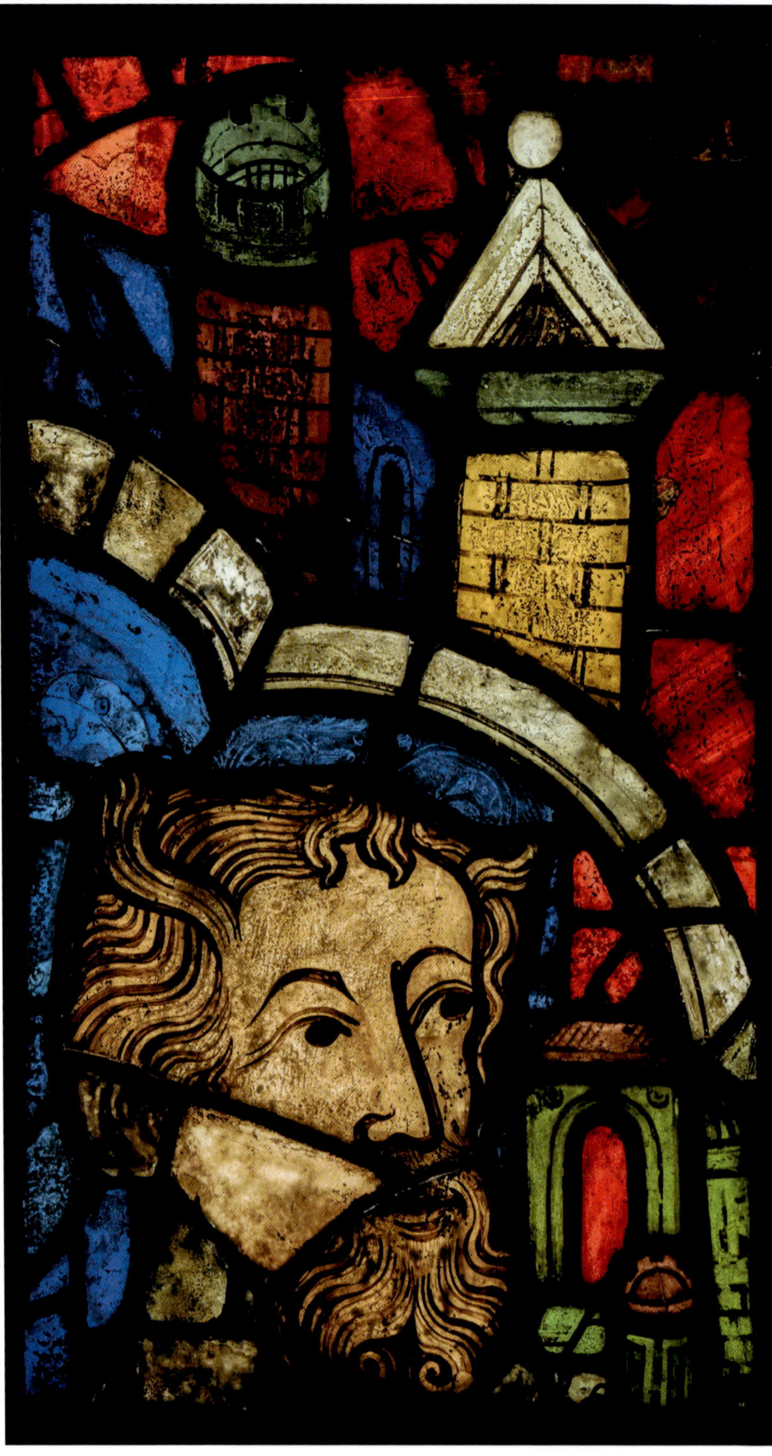

Bearded Head,
possibly Moses,

1170–1400
Made in England and France
Colourless glass, pot metal glass,
vitreous paint, lead
47.1 cm x 27.2 cm x 1 cm
45.1

This panel is a composite of at least
two different windows. The bearded
head is most likely fourteenth-century
English, while the partial architectural
canopy is of earlier, twelfth- or
thirteenth-century French origin.

First documented and illustrated in
the 1840s, when in the collection of
Lord Sidney Herbert (1810–61), the
canopy originally surmounted the
bust of a tonsured saint or beardless
Christ. The panel was subsequently
broken up and the bust installed in
the neo-Romanesque Church of
St Mary and St Nicholas, in Wilton,
Wiltshire (built 1841–45). At Wilton,
the bust's monumental proportions
imply that the canopied figure was
placed in a church's clerestory (the
upper glazed storey) where it would
have been viewed from a distance.

A Feast Scene, 1255–85

Made in France
Colourless glass, pot metal glass, vitreous paint, lead
Overall: 165 cm x 62 cm x 1 cm
Probably made for Clerment-Ferrand Cathedral, France
45.366.a-c

Despite their great age, these three panels depicting a courtly feast and its preparation are remarkably well preserved, with much of the glass, and astonishingly the fragile lead, remaining intact and unrestored after more than 700 years. Burrell, who appreciated authenticity in his collections, regarded this window as amongst his very finest pieces, and used it as a benchmark against which to judge future stained glass acquisitions.

Reputedly from the cathedral of Clermont-Ferrand, France, these windows are comparable in their form, composition, and iconography with the famous glazing scheme of the royal chapel of Sainte-Chapelle, Paris, and may be attributed to the same workshop or associated glaziers.

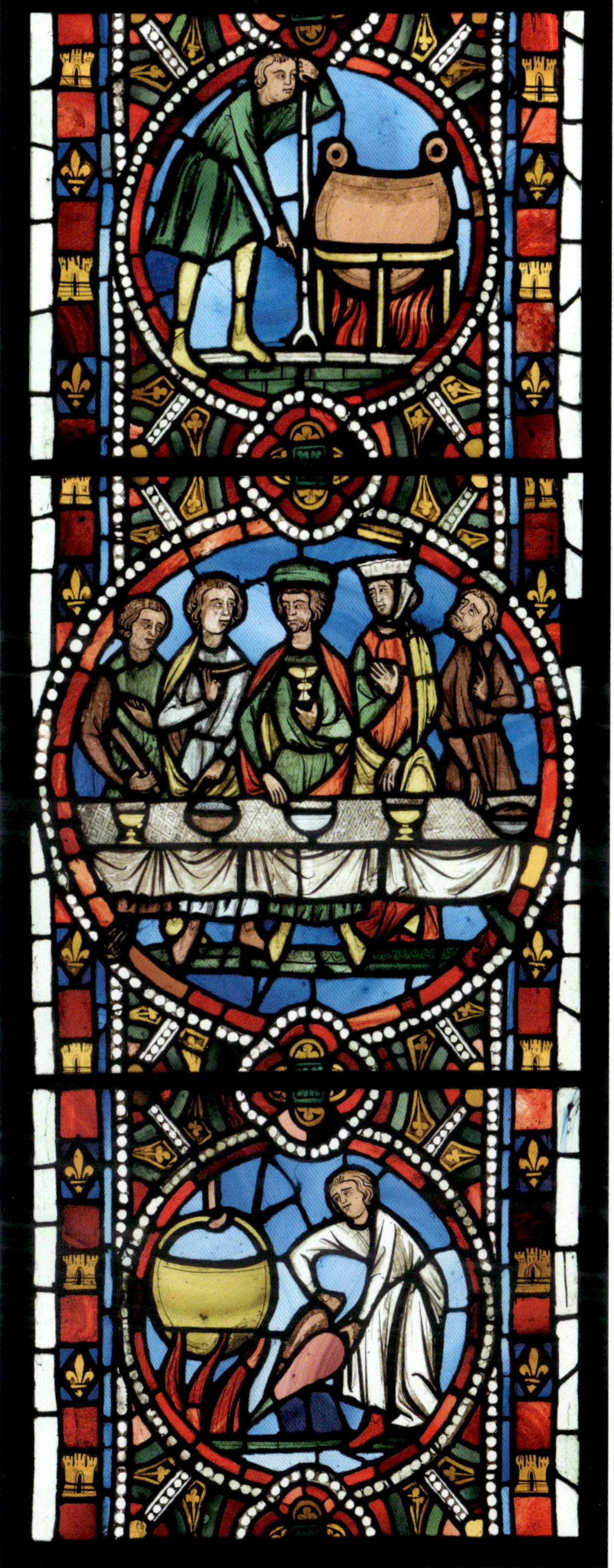

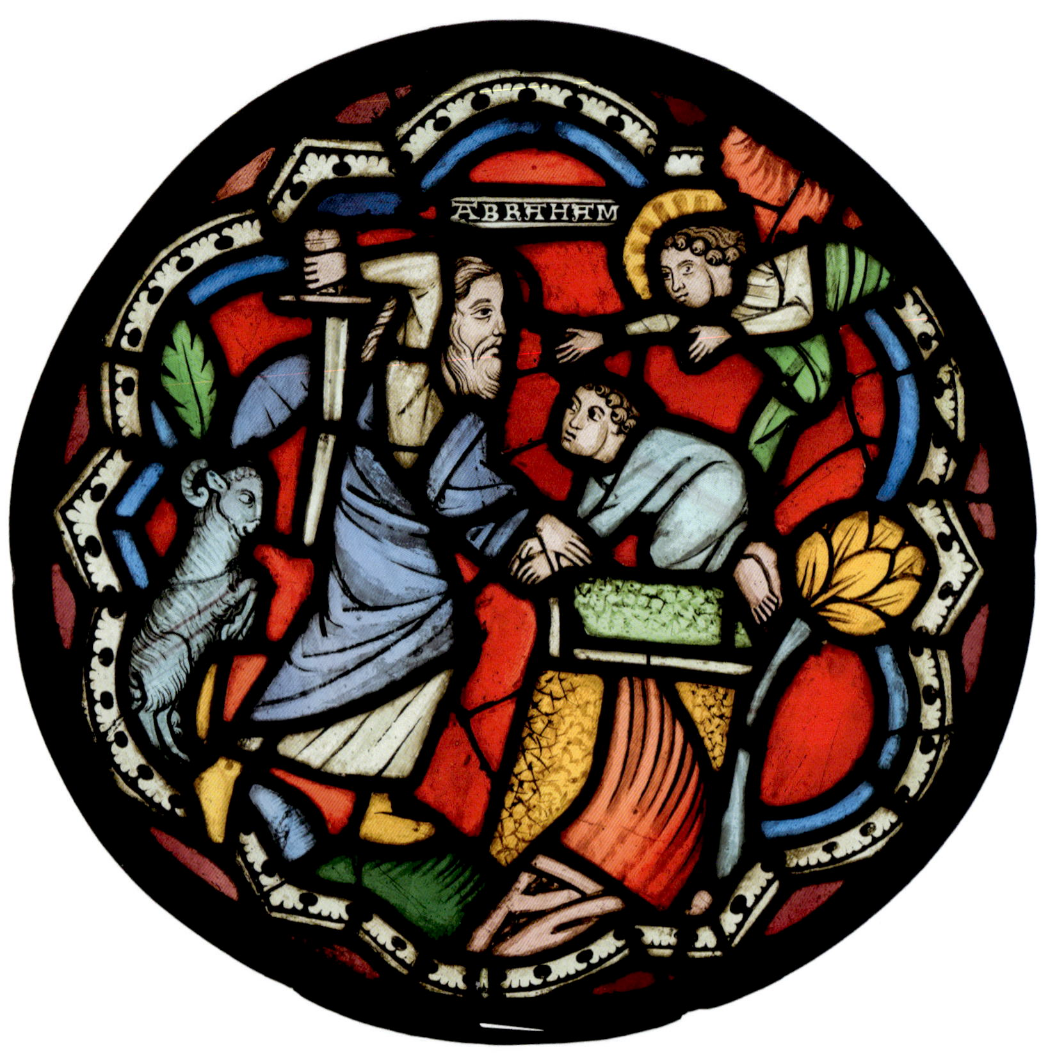

Abraham Prepares to Sacrifice Isaac,
about 1270
Made in Strasbourg, France
Colourless glass, pot metal glass, vitreous paint, lead
46.5 cm x 48.5 cm x 1 cm
Possibly from the Dominican Church, or the Church
of St Thomas at Strasbourg
45.488

In an extraordinary test of his faith, God commanded
Abraham to sacrifice his beloved son Isaac. Here we
see the dramatic culmination of events, as an angel
appears, halting the execution and presenting a ram
to be sacrificed in Isaac's stead. By the thirteenth
century, towering' typological' windows, in which
stories from the Old Testament were presented as
precursors to incidents from the Life and Passion of
Christ, were a well-established means of displaying
biblical narratives. This medallion is understood
to have once flanked an image of the Crucifixion,
drawing parallels between the deliverance of Isaac
(Genesis 22:1–14) and Christ's sacrifice on the cross.

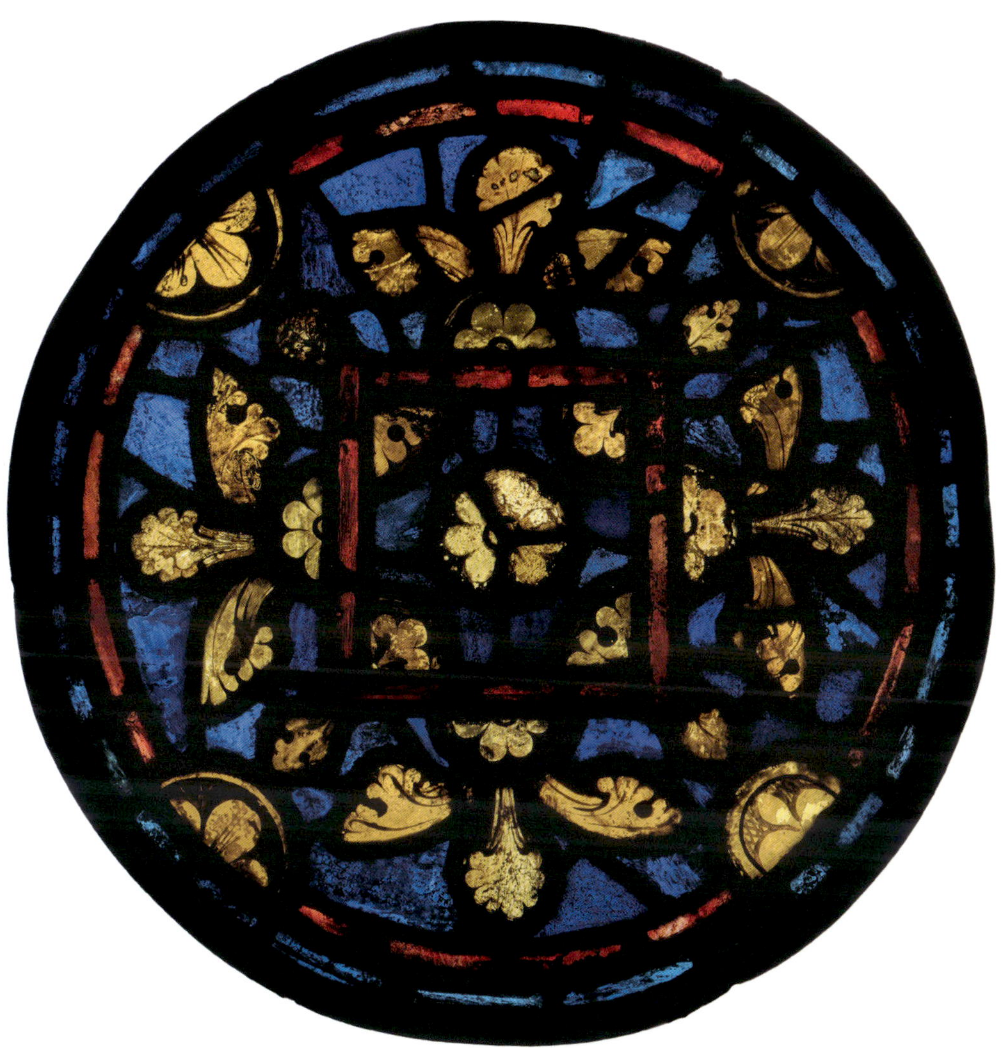

Medallion, 1200–1300
Made in England
Pot metal glass, vitreous paint, lead
44.5 cm x 44.5 cm x 1 cm
45.3

The colours available to glaziers were limited until the fourteenth century, restricted to intense hues of red, blue, yellow, green, purple, and colourless white glass. Known as 'pot metal' glass, the hues of early Gothic glass are the result of metallic oxides introduced to the molten glass during its manufacture. Pot metal red (or 'ruby') initially proved too opaque, and a more translucent alternative was eventually achieved by 'flashing', the process of working red and clear/white glass together, resulting in a thin layer of red over a colourless base. Early experiments with flashing resulted in the distinctive streaked appearance seen in this roundel.

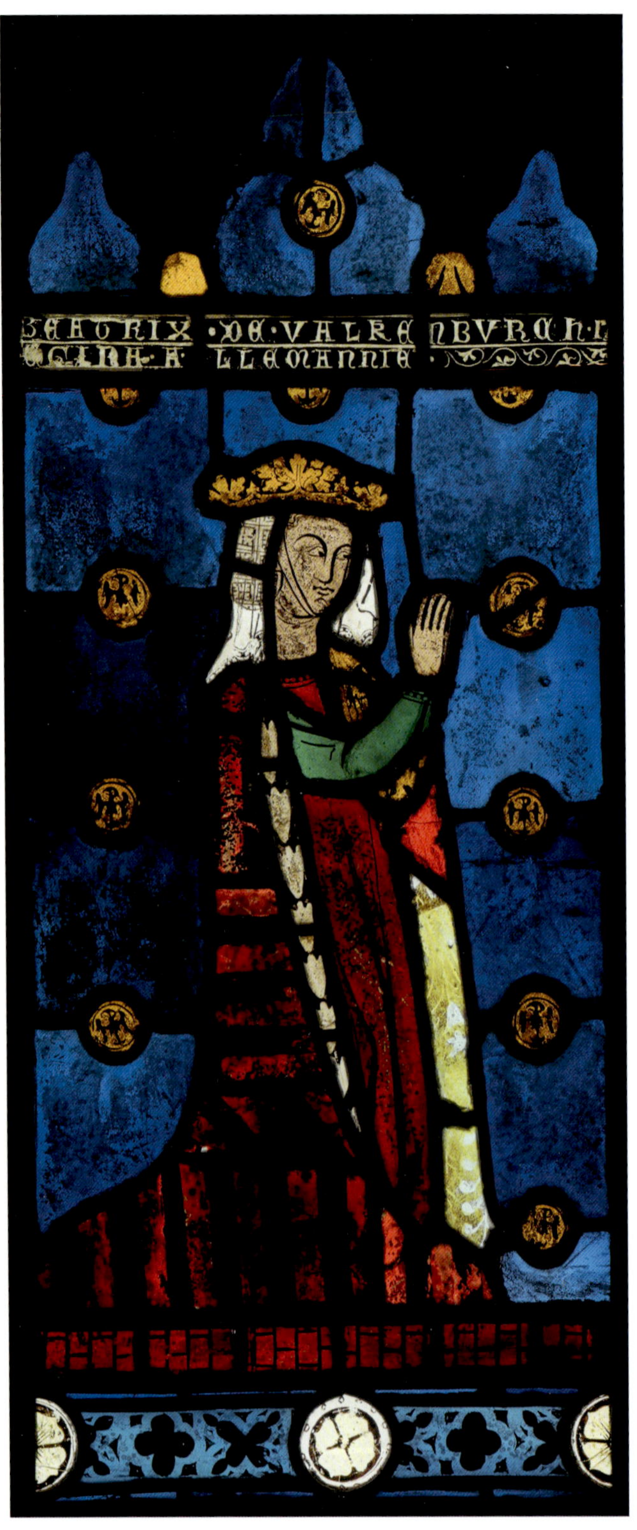

Beatrix of Valkenburg, about 1293
Made in Norwich, England
Colourless glass, pot metal glass, vitreous paint, lead
59.5 cm x 26 cm x 1 cm
Probably from the church of the Greyfriars, Norwich, England
45.2

Beatrix of Valkenburg (about 1254–77) was the third wife of Richard, Earl of Cornwall (1209–72). The younger brother of King Henry III of England (1207–72), Richard was elected as King of the Romans (King of the Germans) in 1257. Beatrix became queen following their marriage in 1269.

This commemorative panel is thought to have been commissioned some years after Beatrix's death, possibly donated to the Franciscan church in Norwich by her nephew, King Edward I (1239–1307). Dating to the late thirteenth century, it is considered one of the earliest intact examples of an English stained glass 'donor portrait' in existence (see p.25).

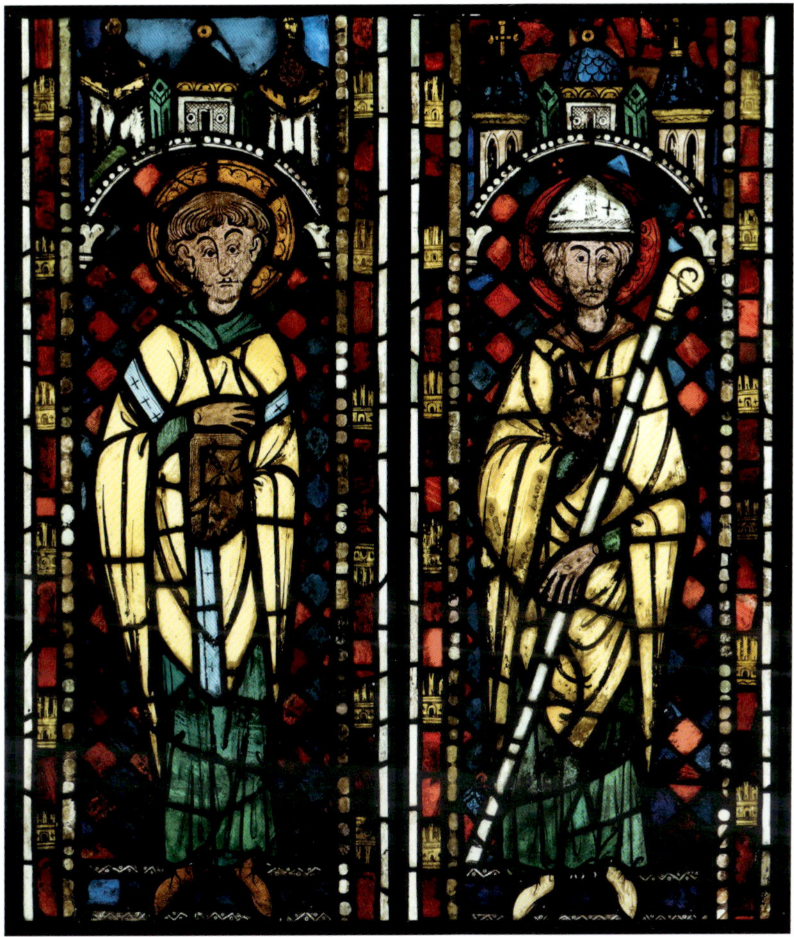

A Priest Saint, possible St Rimbert, and a Bishop Saint, possibly St Nicholas of Myra or St Maternus of Cologne, 1275–1325

Made in Germany
Colourless glass, pot metal glass, vitreous paint, lead
Overall (both): 105 cm x 44 cm x 1 cm
Possibly from the Church of St Materniani and
St Nicolai, Bücken an der Weser, Lower Saxony,
Germany
45.365.1.b, 45.365.2.b

Over the centuries it was not unusual for stained glass windows to be dismantled, repaired, and rebuilt. On occasion, extensive reconstructions were undertaken, perhaps amalgamating broken windows, or reimagining and re-shaping panels in accordance with the changing demands and requirements of their owners.

A photograph from 1914 shows these two figures were once mounted together within a single, smaller round medallion. By the time they were purchased by Burrell in 1939 they were vastly altered, with the figures expanded and divided into two tall lancet windows. The upper and lower portions of this later arrangement, containing abstract decorative passages, have been removed.

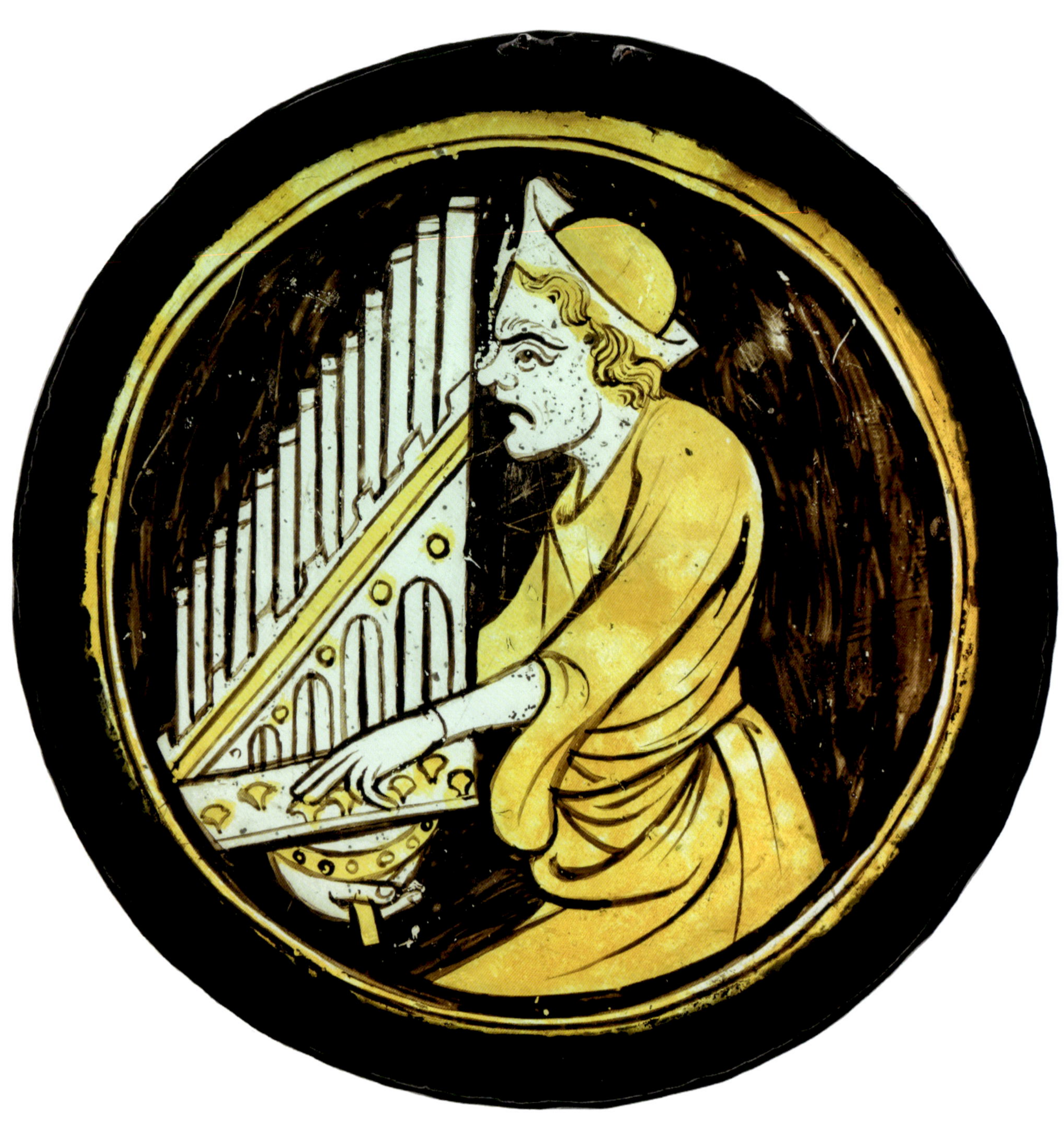

Fourteenth-century Glass

As Gothic architecture matured, window openings became larger and more elaborate. By the fourteenth century, the single lancet windows of the early Gothic period had given way to towering multi-light arrangements, consisting of several narrow openings, separated by slender vertical stone divides (mullions), that rose to terminate in increasingly complex webs of stone tracery. In response to these changes, and faced with a desire for greater illumination, glaziers embraced new approaches to window design and composition, signalling a marked departure from earlier styles.

Moving away from the crowded colour-saturated creations of earlier glazing schemes, in the later thirteenth century, coloured, often figurative, panels of glass were balanced by swathes of sparingly coloured *grisaille*. Figures, once posed in theatrical narrative scenes, were now more commonly painted in elegant, sinuous forms, and presented in isolation below lightly coloured canopies that emulated the window's architectural surrounds.

The dazzling reds and blues that dominated earlier windows were joined by a palette of more earthy tones, including mossy greens, browns, and rich purples. Varying hues of yellow and orange were also introduced, achieved via the application of silver compounds, which imparted colour and stained the glass when fired. The discovery of this 'silver stain' technique revolutionized stained glass,

providing glaziers with a convenient and more economic means of introducing colour and embellishment, without the need for laborious cutting and leading. Blue glass could also be treated with silver stain, producing a range of subtle greens which were often deployed in landscapes.

Sir William's first known acquisition of stained glass can be dated to 1892, when the 31-year-old Burrell commissioned a window by the versatile Glasgow-born designer and architect George Walton (1867–1933). Executed in a decorative Art and Crafts style, Walton's design on the theme of *Gather Ye Rosebuds While Ye May*, presents a romantic and highly stylized scene of young women amongst a dream-like landscape and floral motifs. Installed in the stairhead of 4 Devonshire Gardens, the Glasgow home Burrell shared throughout the 1890s with his mother Isabella (1834–1912), the glass remains in situ, although the lower panels have subsequently been lost. This window was Burrell's only contemporary stained glass commission, perhaps suggesting that his tastes in the medium were still formulating at the time of its undertaking.

It is also during this period that Burrell is understood to have begun procuring historic stained glass, examples of which were loaned to the 1901 Glasgow International Exhibition. The exhibition catalogue reveals a modest assemblage of mostly sixteenth- and seventeenth-century domestic and heraldic glass, likely corresponding with the Dutch, Swiss, and German panels and roundels that were installed in 8 Great Western Terrace, Burrell's first marital home, purchased in 1901. In the 1940s, Burrell, by then a more experienced collector, dispensed with many of these early acquisitions, labelling them as 'unimportant' and 'moderate in quality'.

Executed on a single piece of clear glass, this charming roundel dating from 1335–50 demonstrates the new possibilities presented by the discovery of silver stain. Cheaper than traditionally cut and leaded glass, silver stained and painted panels became ubiquitous in the following centuries. (45.27, see p.28)

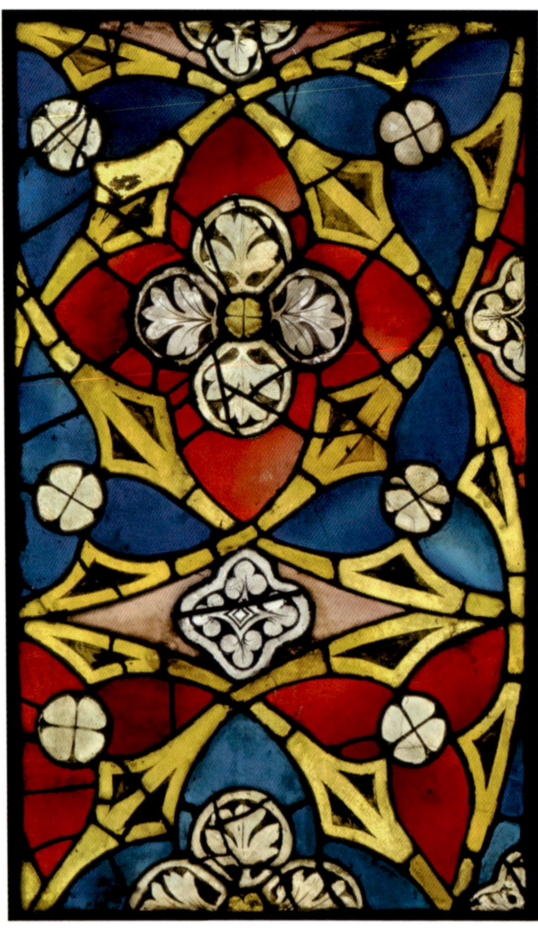 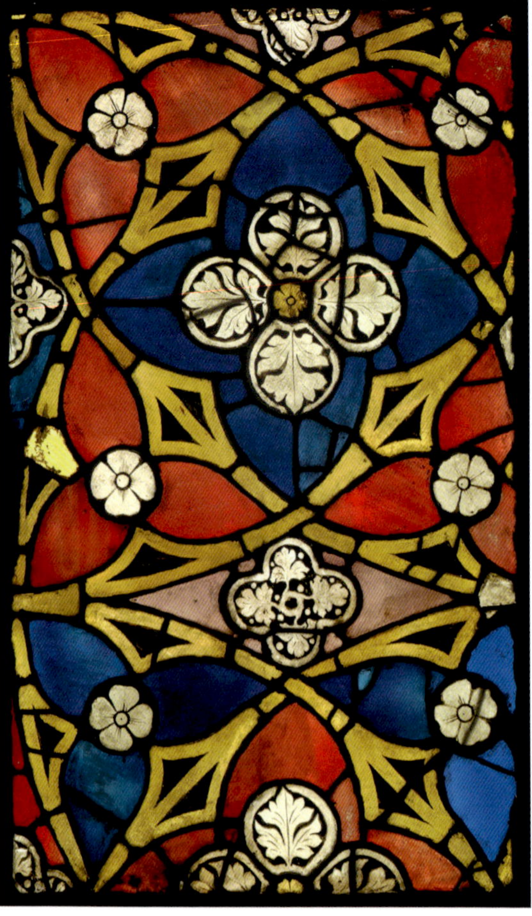

Ornamental panels, about 1300

Made in Erfurt, Germany
Colourless glass, pot metal glass, vitreous paint, lead
90.2 cm x 57.2 cm x 1 cm
88.9 cm x 53.3 cm X 1 cm
Removed from the Church of St Augustine's
Monastery, Erfurt, Thuringia, Germany
45.482, 45.483

Known as '*tapetenfester*' (carpet windows), highly ornamental non-figurative windows are found in several church glazing schemes from late thirteenth- and early fourteenth-century Germany. Presenting a kaleidoscope of colour, these decorative pieces were originally installed in the choir of the Augustinian church in Erfurt, where they constituted part of a repetitive geometric arrangement across two slender lancet windows.

Subject to numerous repairs, the restored windows at Erfurt contain little authentic medieval glass and are largely composed of modern replacements, although the attractive design is true to the original. These two panels were removed during an extensive restoration programme undertaken in the 1930s.

Royal Arms of England, 1300–25
Made in England
Pot metal glass, vitreous paint, lead
29 cm x 29 cm x 1 cm
45.129

A keen collector of items with noble and royal associations, Burrell was pleased to secure this 'very fine… and early' heraldic medallion from the collection of the physician and antiquarian Philip Nelson (1872–1953) in 1946.

This shield is charged with the royal arms of England; the addition of the blue, decorative, strap-like detail, known as a 'label of three points' in heraldry, identifies these as the arms of the monarch's eldest son and heir. On the grounds of composition and style the medallion is dated to the early fourteenth century, suggesting that the shield is representative of either Edward II (1284–1327) or his son, Edward III (1312–77), prior to their ascendancy to the throne.

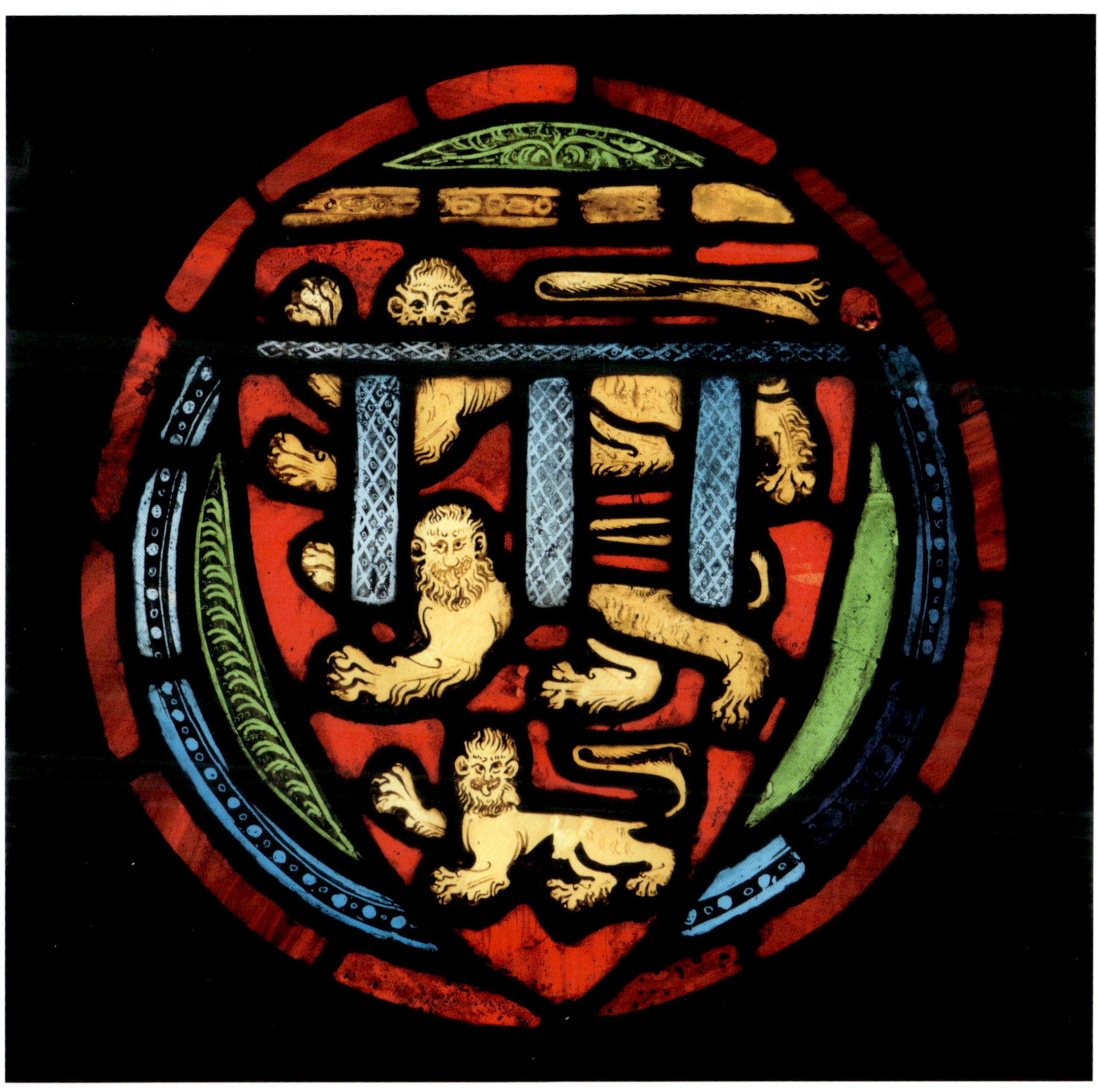

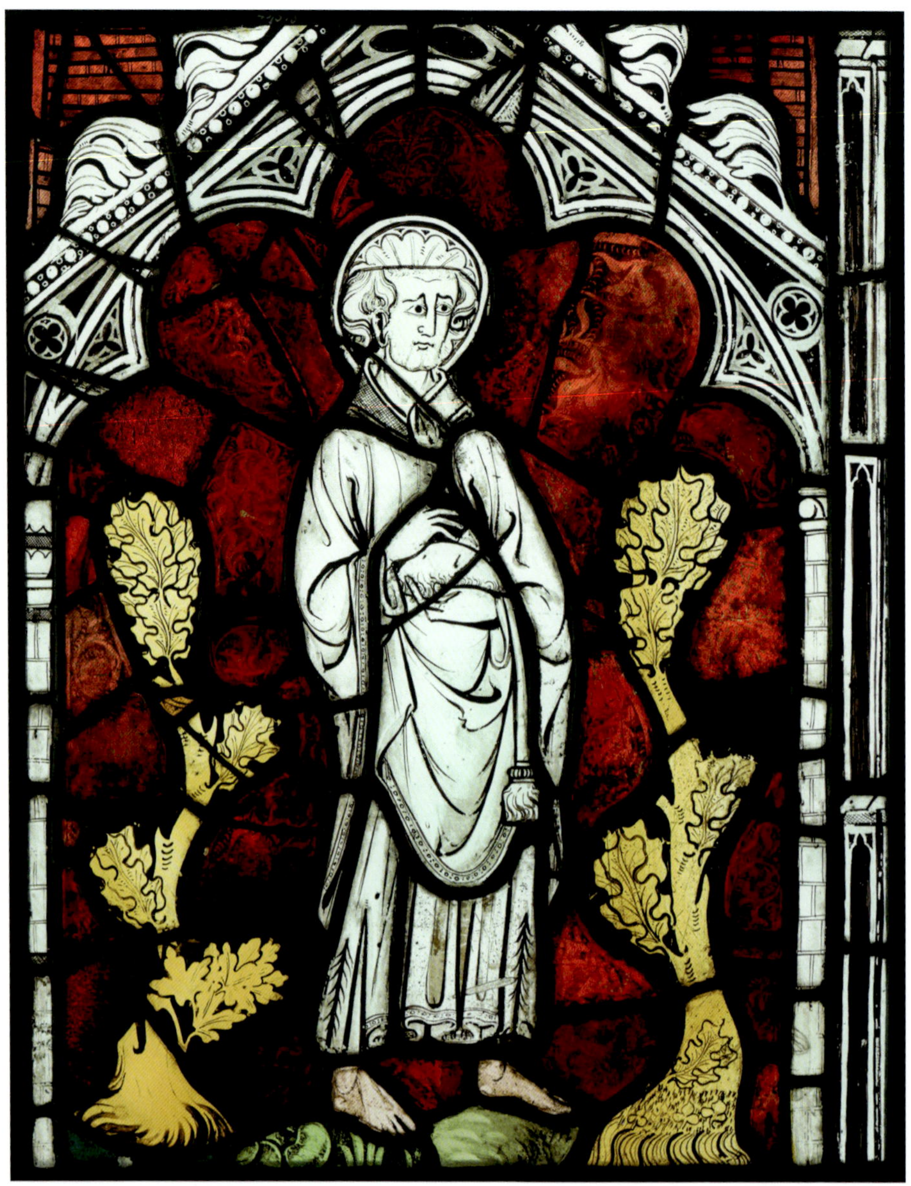

St Nicasius of Rheims and St Clement of Rome, 1300–1400

Possibly made in France
Colourless glass, pot metal glass, vitreous paint, silver stain, lead
64 cm x 49 cm x 1 cm
64 cm x 50 cm x 1 cm
45.373, 45.374

Set against a diapered red backdrop in contrasting white *grisailles*, St Nicasius (d. either 407 or 451 AD) and St Clement (d. about 100 AD), are framed within complementary shrine-like architectural surrounds. Nicasius, Bishop of Rheims, holds the crown of his own head, which by tradition was severed when the city was sacked by an invading force in the fifth century. St Clement, Bishop of Rome, is identified by the anchor chained around his neck as he is thrown into the sea. Said to have been banished

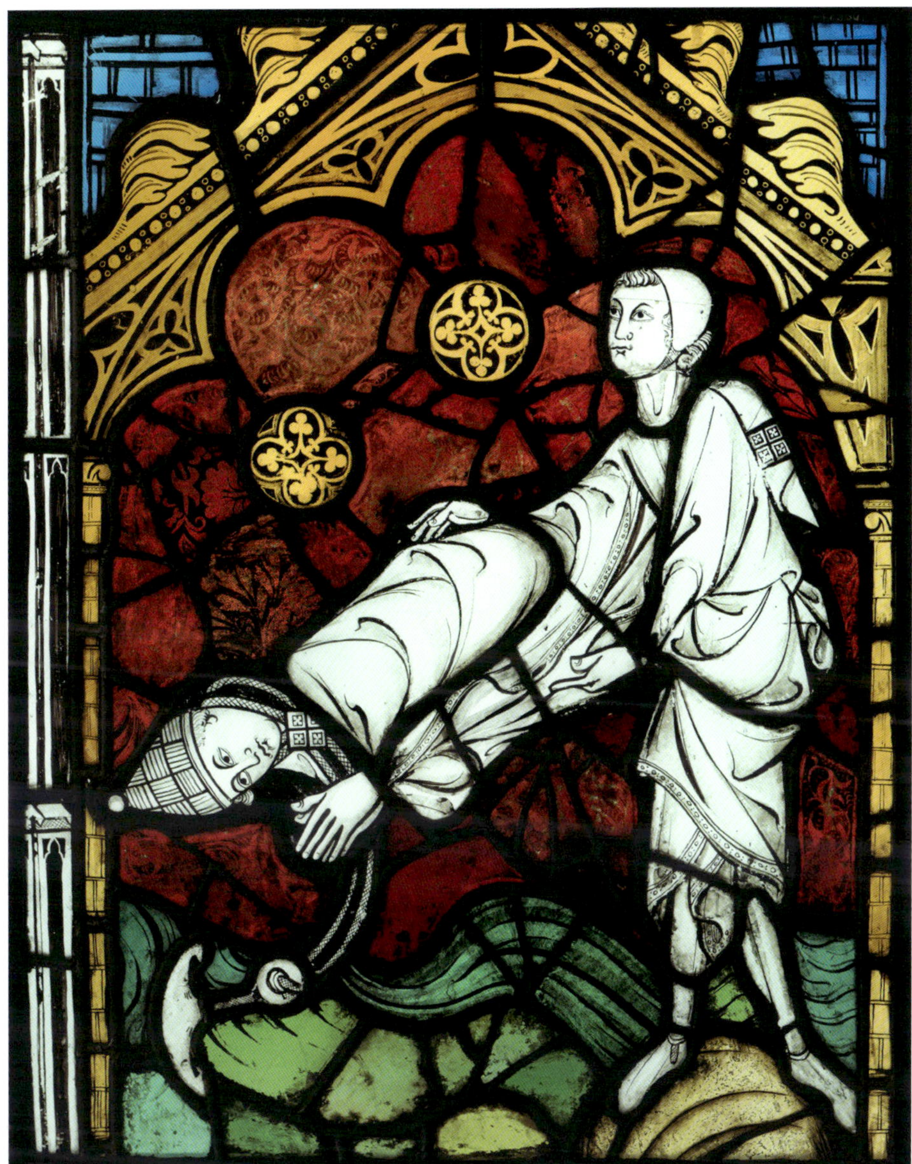

from Rome by the Emperor Trajan (53–117 AD), Clement was drowned while in exile at Chersonesus, an ancient city in the Crimean Peninsula.

Burrell purchased these panels via the dealers Thomas and Drake, who originally intended to sell them on the more lucrative American market. Regarded as the firm's 'finest Gothic panels', they were initially offered to Burrell in 1938 for £750, a price that dealer Wilfred Drake commented was 'less than half' of that quoted to the Metropolitan Museum of Art, New York. In pursuit of an even greater bargain, Burrell refused the offer. In January 1940, having failed to sell the panels to the Washington National Cathedral, Washington D.C., Drake again approached Burrell, who eventually acquired the pair for the much-reduced sum of £450.

The Virgin Mary and St John the Baptist, about 1320

Made in Switzerland
Colourless glass, pot metal glass, vitreous paint, lead
79.7 cm x 23.5 cm x 1 cm
80.1 cm x 23.3 cm x 1 cm
45.480.a-b

These two small panels are likely to have once comprised part of a three-panel arrangement representing the Last Judgement. The central panel, now missing, may have depicted an enthroned Christ, seated in judgement over the souls of the dead. The Virgin Mary and St John the Baptist would have flanked this central image, kneeling with their hands clasped in prayer and supplication towards the now-missing Christ – appealing to Him and interceding on behalf of the resurrected souls who can be seen below.

These panels' modest dimensions suggest that the window they formed was perhaps intended for a small chapel or a village church.

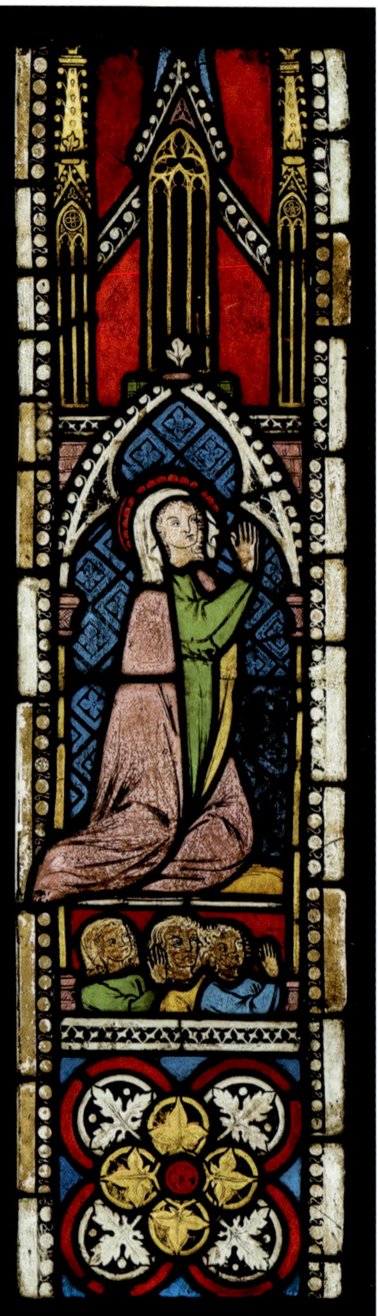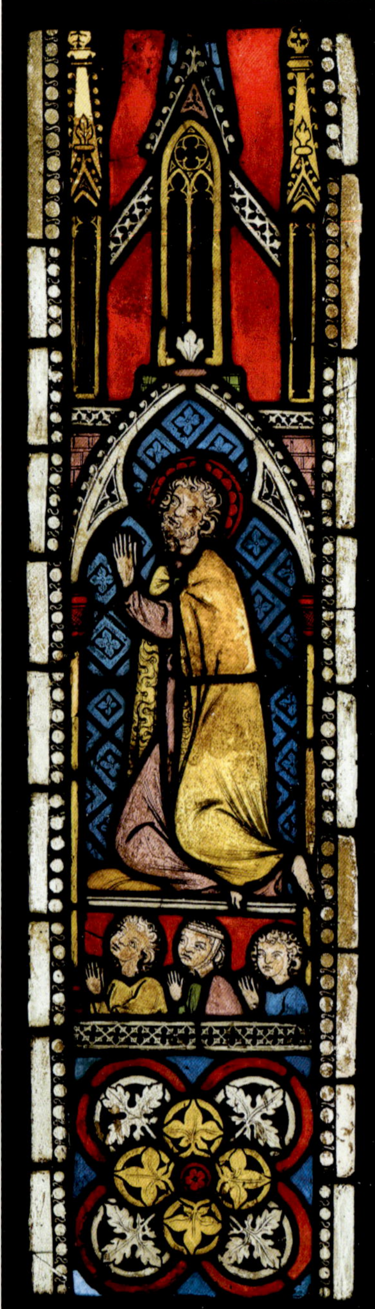

Kneeling Donor, 1350–1400

Made in England
Colourless glass, pot metal glass,
vitreous paint, silver stain, lead
54.7 cm x 35 cm x 1 cm
45.9

During the Middle Ages, churches
relied on the munificence of donors
to finance building work and enrich
their interiors. Motivated by their
piety, concerns for their souls'
salvation, and a desire to be
remembered in the prayers of the
community, prosperous patrons
could commission expensive
stained glass featuring their family's
heraldic arms, or even portraits,
as reminders of their generosity,
wealth, and status.

The donor and source of this piece
are not known, although the details
are strikingly similar to a panel
commemorating William and Matilda
Cele, attributed to a parish church
in Suffolk, now in the collection of
the Victoria and Albert Museum,
London. The text below appears
unrelated and seemingly refers
to the parishioners of Gresford,
Denbighshire, Wales. It says *p(ar)
ichianoru(m) de Gresford / iari
fecerunt de suis*, meaning 'the
parishioners of Gresford made this
themselves.'

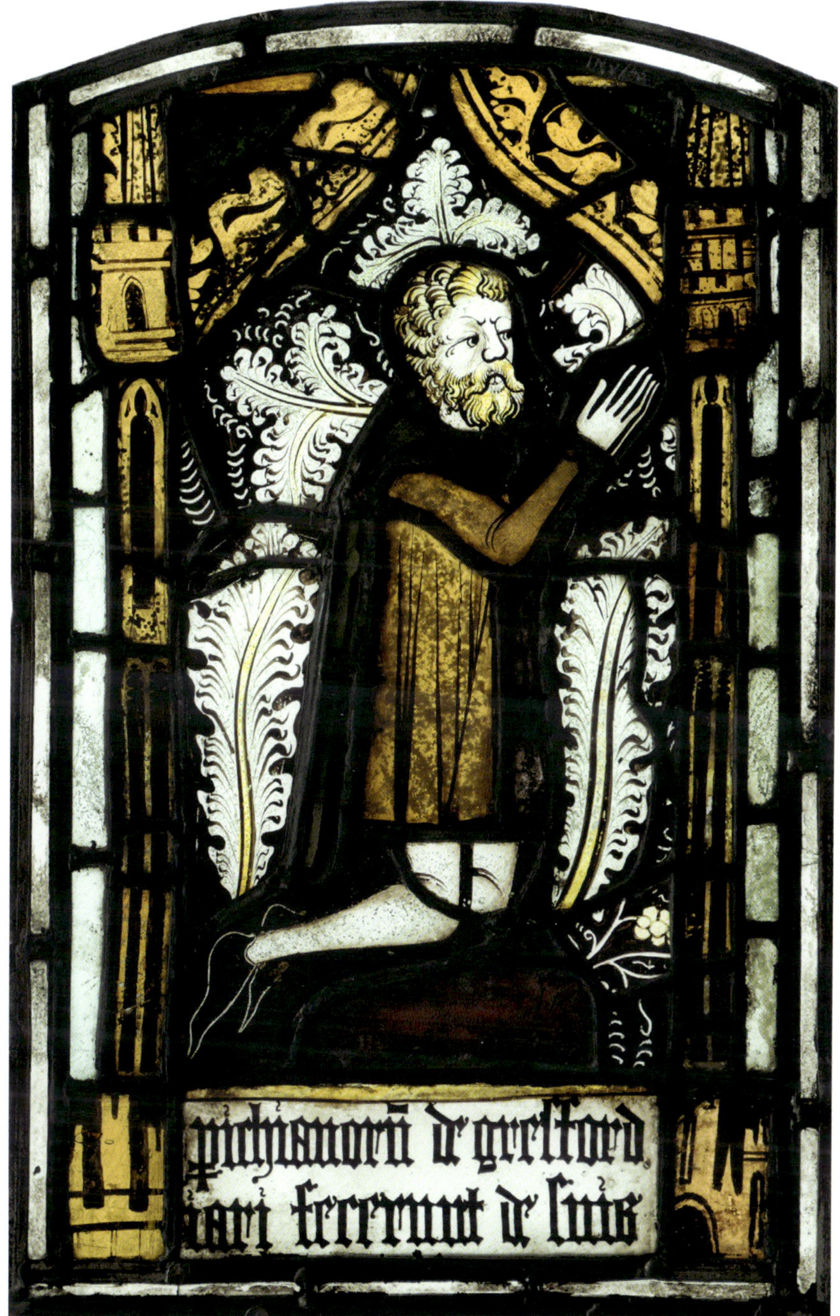

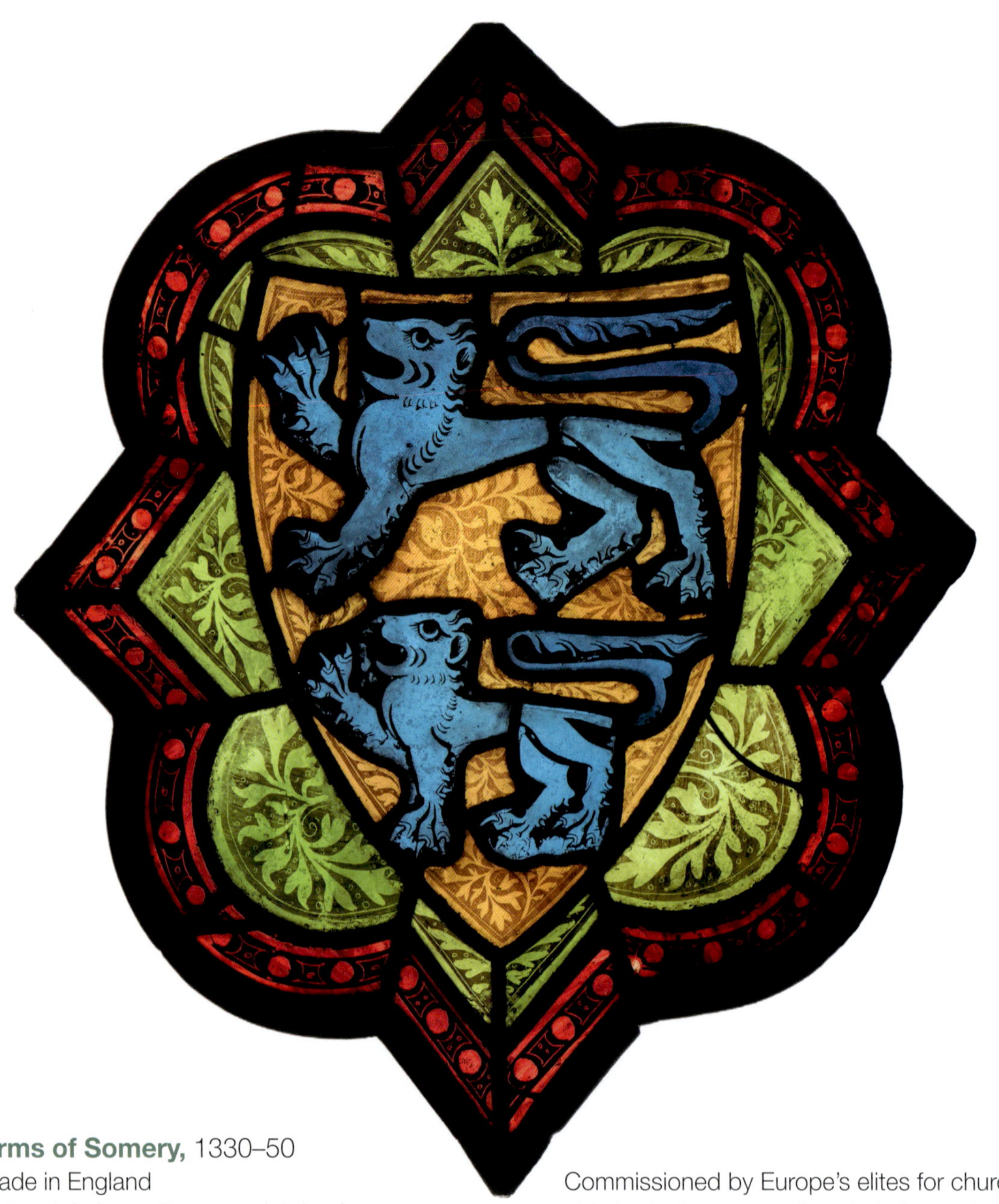

Arms of Somery, 1330–50
Made in England
Pot metal glass, vitreous paint, lead
50.5 cm x 43 cm x 1 cm
45.109

With its eye-catching colour and use of bold lines, stained glass proved an especially suitable medium for the presentation of heraldic arms – recognition of which relied on a limited palette of high-contrast colours and distinctive legible devices or motifs.

Commissioned by Europe's elites for churches and civic institutions, as well as their domestic residences, armorial glass served as a public demonstration of familial lineage and social rank.

This shield bears the arms of the Somery family of Dudley Castle in the West Midlands. Embellished with scrolling foliate details scratched through a thin wash of paint, this glass is amongst Burrell's oldest and most elegantly executed heraldic panels.

St Mary of Egypt, 1300–30

Made in France
Pot metal glass, vitreous paint, lead
86.4 cm x 29.7 cm x 1 cm
45.369

Drawn with great sensitivity, this portrait of St Mary of Egypt displays the painter's masterful use of shadow to create a soft and contoured beauty to Mary's face. Her long hair cascades in thick waves, covering her whole body, as she clasps her hands in penitence.

Tradition dictates that Mary was a prostitute, who, upon her conversion, withdrew to the desert to pursue a hermit's life of penance and contemplation. In time her clothes wore out and fell away, leaving only her flowing hair to cover her nakedness. Mary's cult was particularly popular in France. It forms the subject of glazing schemes at both Chartres and Bourges cathedrals.

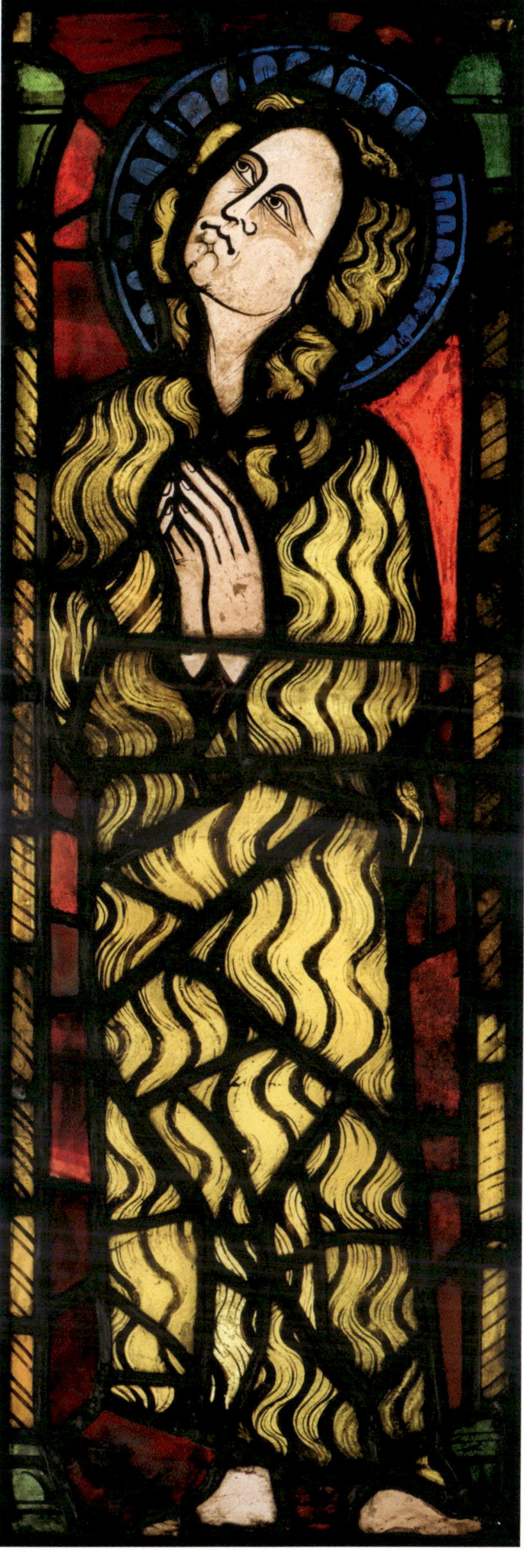

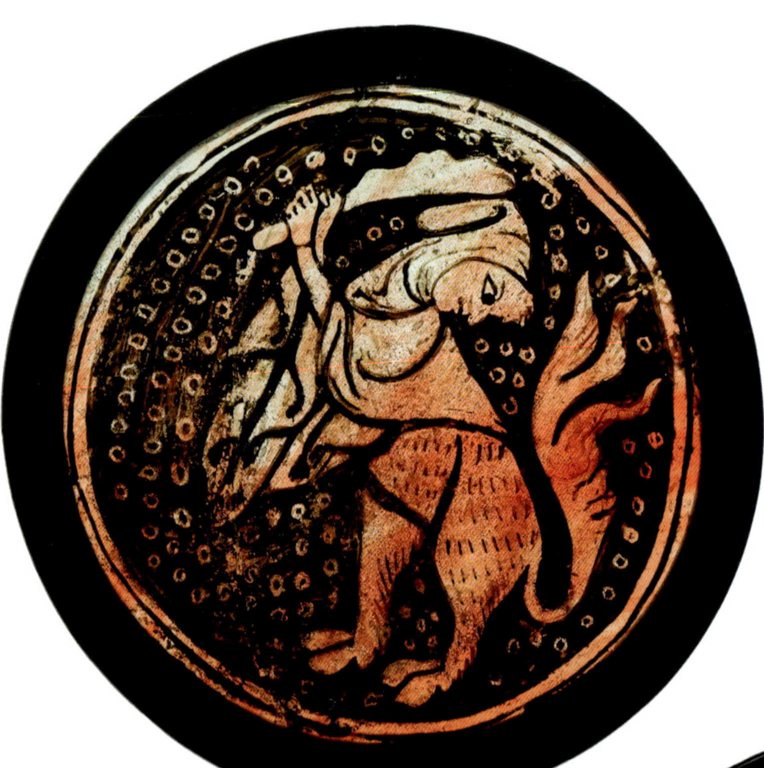

Hybrid Man-Animal,
about 1325–50
Made in England
Pot metal glass, vitreous paint, lead
15.7 cm x 15.7 cm x 1 cm
45.17

Man Playing Organ,
about 1335–50
Made in York, England, attributed to
the workshop of Master Robert
Colourless glass, vitreous paint, silver
stain, lead
15.8 cm x 15.8 cm x 1 cm
45.27

These playful and amusing fourteenth-century roundels can be compared with *drolleries,* the often-humorous vignettes of fantastical beasts and beguiling figures that inhabited the margins of medieval manuscripts and prayer books.

Such figures are frequently encountered in the decorative schemes of medieval churches, and there has been much debate as to how this secular imagery should be interpreted. Whether purely decorative, moralizing, or allegorical, they are often intentionally comical.

The slouched, grimacing, organ player was perhaps intended as a light-hearted parody, inviting good-humoured comparisons with the beautiful and composed musical angels that adorned church interiors (see p.44).

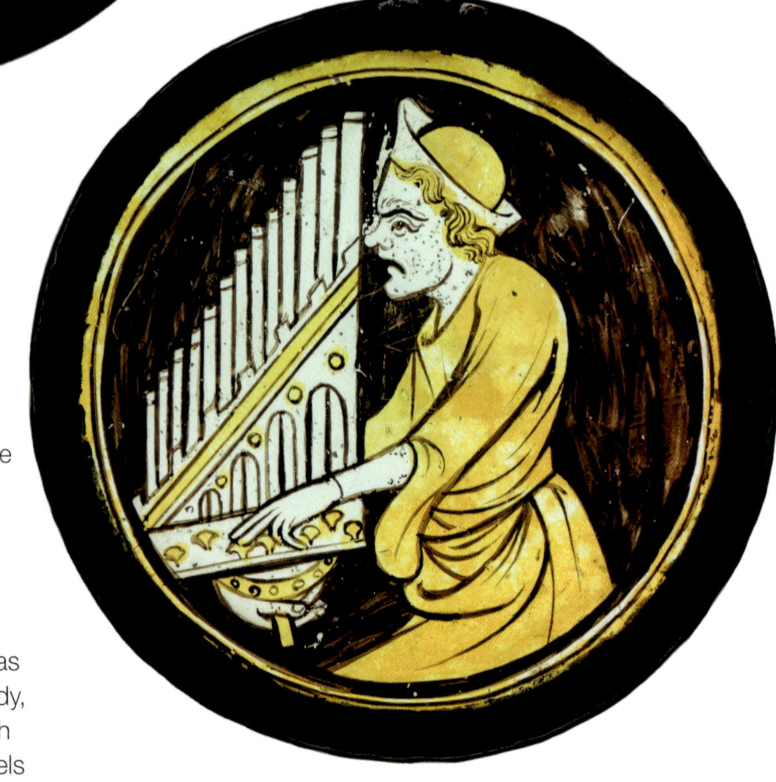

Arms of John de Haudlo (Hadlow), 1325–75

Made in England
Colourless glass, pot metal glass, vitreous paint,
silver stain, lead
43.8 cm x 47 cm x 1 cm
45.111

This exquisite armorial panel was displayed in 1918
at a London exhibition of stained glass held by the
artist and dealer George Grosvenor Thomas (1856–
1923). It was acquired by Thomas from Stowe Park,
Buckinghamshire, where it was installed in a
decorative garden folly. The Gothic Temple, built in
1741, was an influential early example of the Gothic
revivalist style that came to dominate Victorian British
architecture. The panel's medieval origins remain
unknown.

Representing the arms of Sir John de Haudlo of
Boarstall, Buckinghamshire (about 1271–1346),
the precisely placed golden droplets (or *gouttes,*
as they are termed in heraldry) highlight the great
intricacy that could be achieved by fourteenth-
century glaziers.

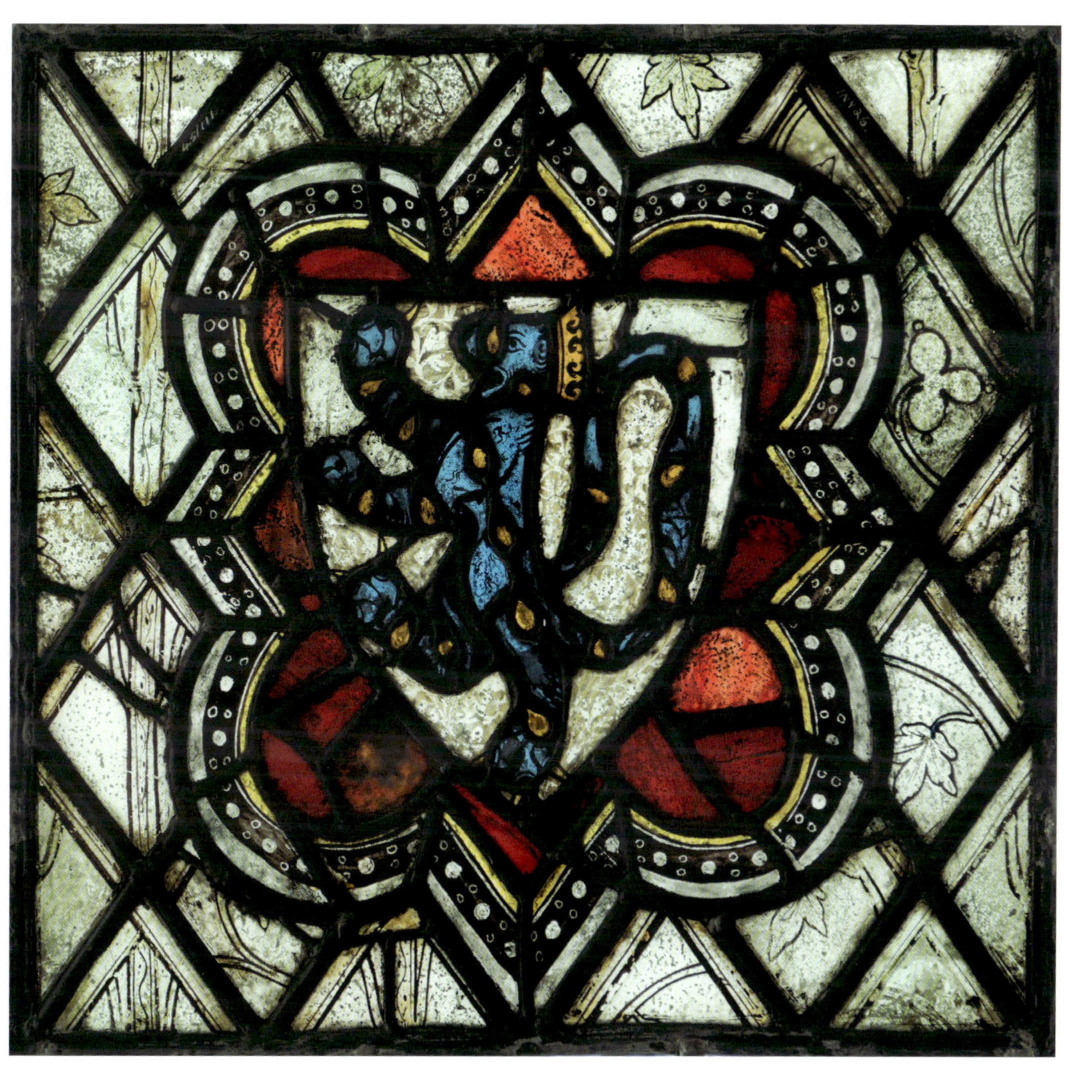

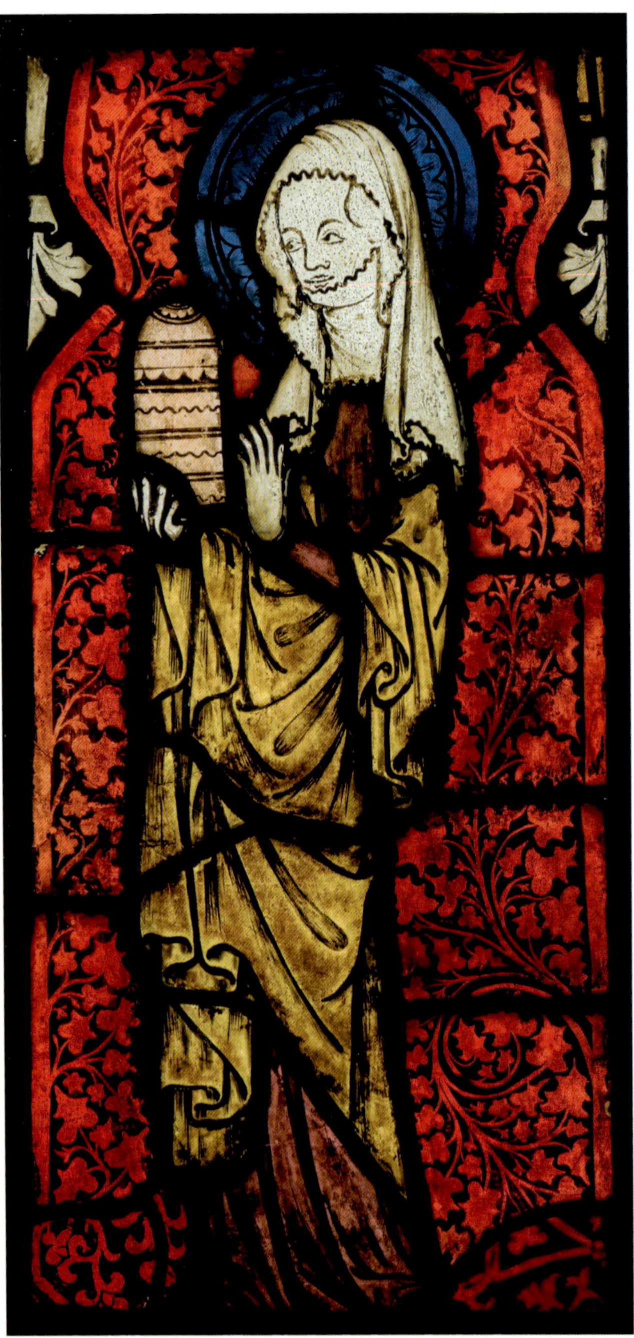

St Mary Magdalene, about 1350
Probably made in Constance, Switzerland
Colourless glass, pot metal glass, vitreous paint, lead
47.5 cm x 23.5 cm x 1 cm
From the Liebfrauenkirche in Meßkirch, Switzerland
45.479

Standing against a richly foliated red backcloth,
the figure of St Mary Magdalene is identified by
the ointment jar she holds in her right hand. She is
traditionally associated with the unnamed sinful
woman of the Gospel of Luke (7:36-50), who
anointed the feet of Christ with precious ointment
in an act of penance and devotion.

This panel is one of only three windows known to
have survived from the choir of the Liebfrauenkirche
in Meßkirch, north of Lake Constance. Mary is
presented as a beautiful and fashionably attired
young woman. Her dress, including the barbet,
a cloth worn over the chin and veil, date this panel
to the mid-fourteenth century.

Virgin Mary and the Christ Child, 1300–1400
Made in France or Germany
Pot metal glass, vitreous paint, silver stain, lead
96 cm x 37.5 cm x 1 cm
45.371

The Virgin Mary was the subject of universal devotion
throughout medieval Christendom. She was
considered the most powerful intercessor between
God and humankind. Innumerable works of art in
honour and praise of the Virgin filled public and
private spaces, including stained glass windows
dedicated to her image and episodes from her life.

Here the Virgin is shown as the Queen of Heaven,
crowned, and clothed in rich, sumptuous fabrics.
Cradled in her left arm, the Infant Christ gazes up
at his mother while tenderly caressing her chin.
Between them they hold an apple, symbolic of their
redemptive role as the new Adam and Eve.

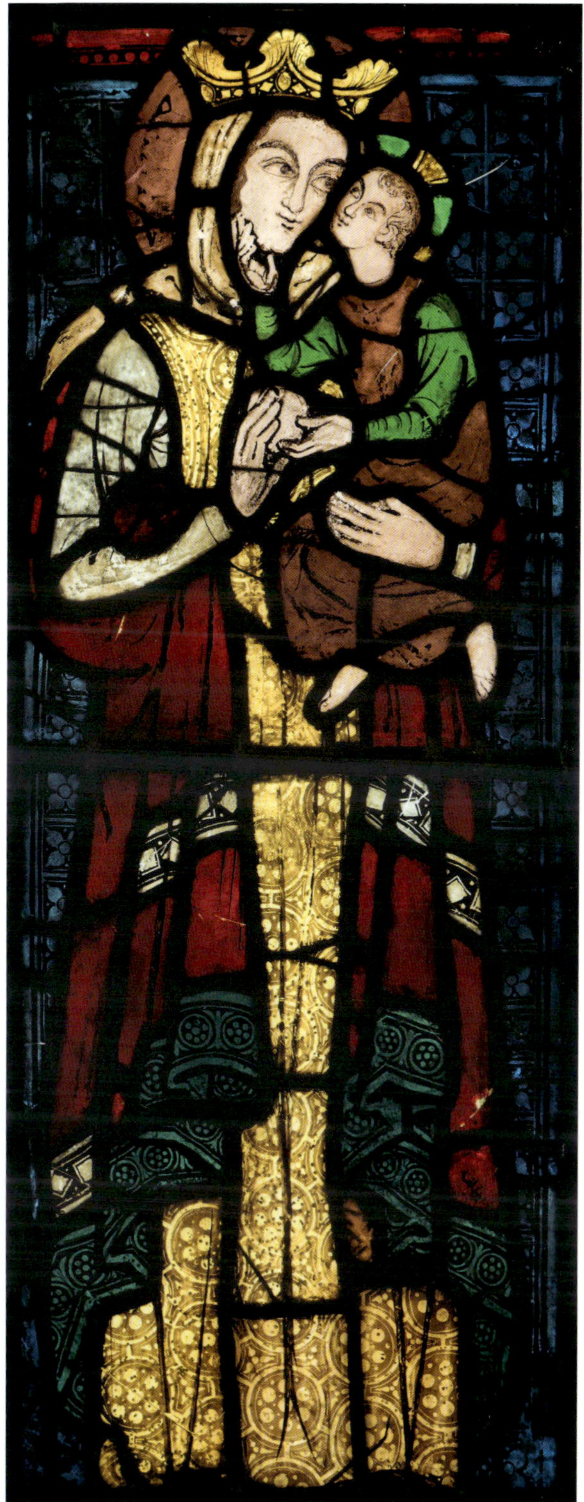

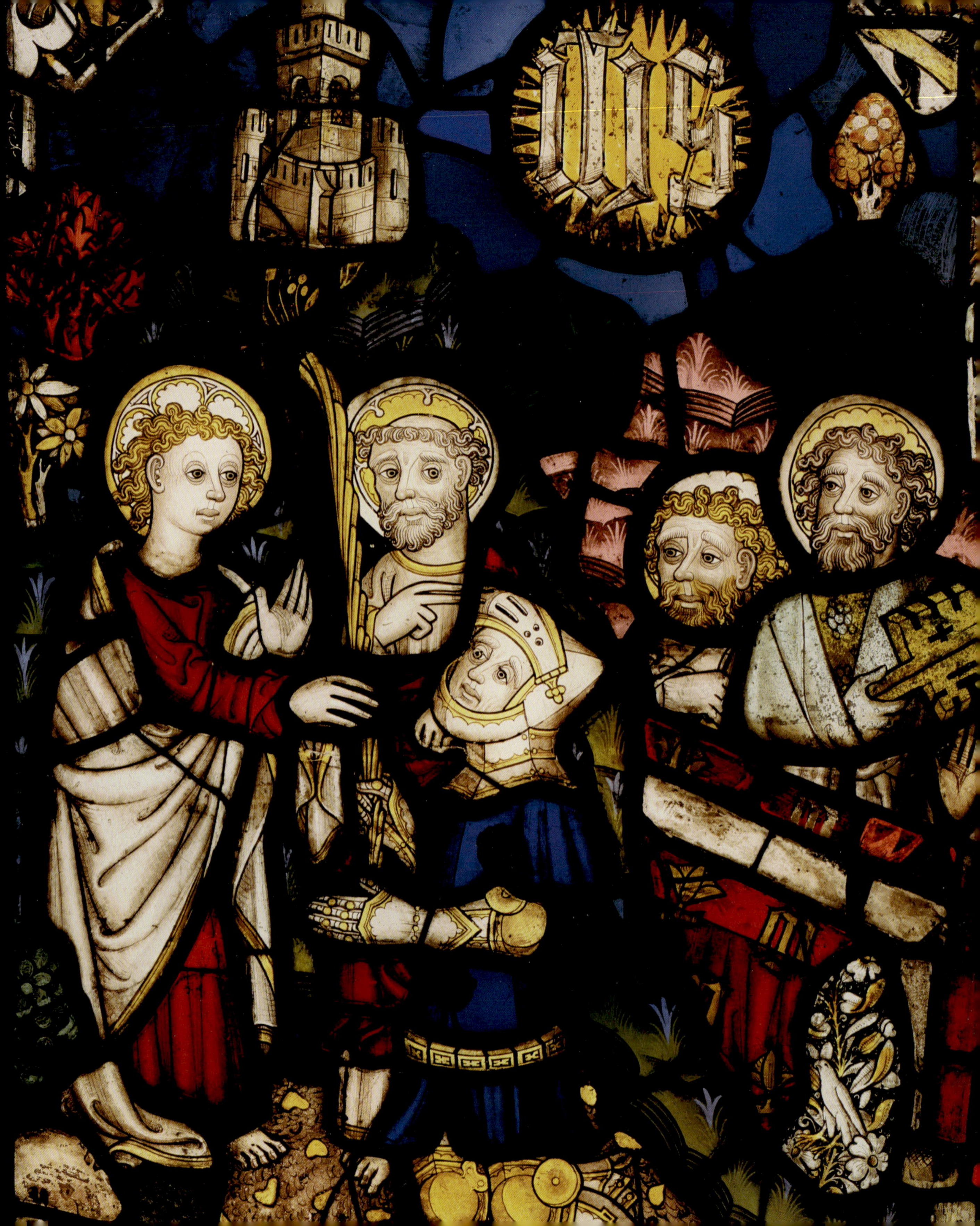

Fifteenth-century Glass

The popularity of stained glass continued unabated into the fifteenth century, with great glazing schemes erected throughout Europe for both new and established religious houses.

By the 1400s, the burgeoning professional classes had emerged as important new patrons of the arts, pouring their growing resources into lavish glazing schemes for their private chapels and local churches. Narrative windows were painted with lively imagery, including the extraordinary events of saints' lives and the Joys and Sorrows of Christ and the Virgin. Such scenes were once again in vogue, appealing to the popular religious interests and devotional needs of these new patrons and the laity of the parish.

Stained glass artists began modelling figures in softer, more realistic forms, painting faces with characterful and distinct features that evoked real life. The influence of Renaissance art and contemporary Netherlandish panel painting is increasingly evident from the middle of the century, with stained glass design and execution drawing ever closer to conventional painting with its emphasis on naturalism, detail and perspective. By the latter part of the 1400s, the canopy and figure form established in the fourteenth century was gradually being abandoned, and glass painters began to show growing disregard for the divisions imposed by the window's mullions, producing expansive scenes that ran across several lights. Secular stained glass became more prevalent during this century, with heraldic panels, quarries (see p.66), and small figurative roundels, becoming customary in churches, public buildings, and wealthier domestic residences.

Having accrued a significant fortune from the sale of much of his shipping fleet during World War I, Burrell and his wife Constance, Lady Burrell, acquired Hutton Castle near Berwick-upon-Tweed in the Borders in 1916. Burrell's expenditure on new acquisitions rose considerably following the purchase of Hutton, with substantial sums spent on renovations and the procurement of medieval and Renaissance treasures, including stained glass, to furnish the castle's rich Gothic interiors.

An unpublished 1932 catalogue of the stained glass collection reveals the astonishing extent of Hutton's glazing scheme. In total, some 250 ancient windows and panels were liberally incorporated throughout the building, appearing not only in the Burrells' living and entertaining spaces but, unusually, within the windows of servants' quarters, butlers' and maids' staircases, service corridors, and even pantries, areas that Burrell would have had little cause to frequent.

Opposite: Demonstrating a range of techniques, passages of red flashed glass in this panel have been skilfully abraded, with the top red layer ground away to expose the colourless glass below. Further treated with silver stain, the red drapery appears as though woven with decorative golden accents. (Detail of 45.92, see p.43)

Religious, secular, and heraldic panels,

about 1400
Made in Germany, probably in Lower Saxony
Colourless glass, pot metal glass, vitreous paint,
silver stain, lead
69.5 cm x 49.6 cm x 1 cm
69.5 cm x 50 cm x 1 cm
69.5 cm x 50 cm x 1 cm
70.7 cm x 50.4 cm x 1 cm
45.486.1.b, 45.486.2.a, 45.486.6.a, 45.486.1.a

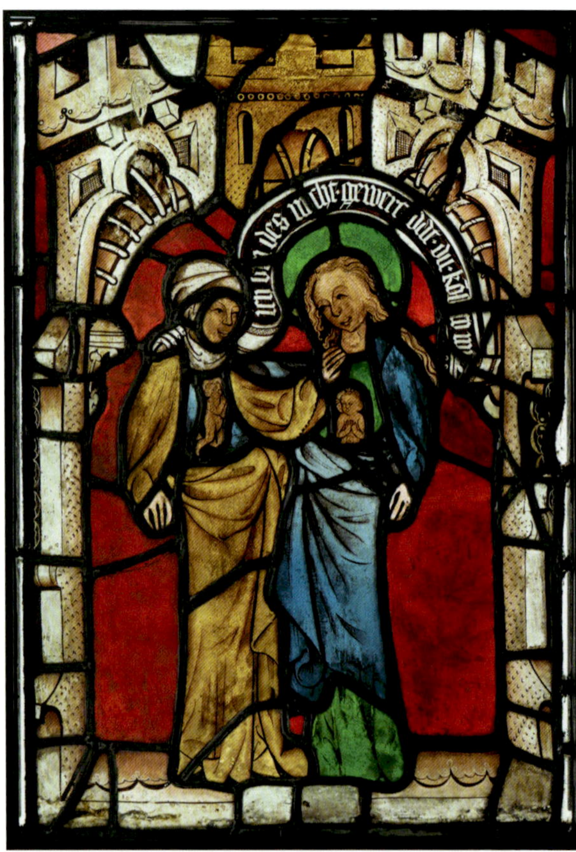

This attractive panel represents the Visitation, the
meeting of cousins St Elizabeth and the Virgin Mary
while pregnant with St John the Baptist and Christ,
respectively. Linguistic evidence taken from this
panel is suggestive of a north German origin.
(45.486.2.a)

These panels come from a series of 12 purchased
by Burrell in 1939 through the dealers Frank Partridge
and Sons Ltd. They were previously in the collection
of the American newspaper tycoon William Randolph
Hearst (1863–1951). Hearst's archives state that
they came from an unidentified castle in Sweden,
although their origin is likely German.

The panels are diverse in nature and include heraldic,
religious, and secular themes. An intriguing sequence
of five panels portraying rural and working life was
possibly commissioned by confraternities or guilds
of working people to beautify their local religious
institution, thereby signifying their important presence
within the community.

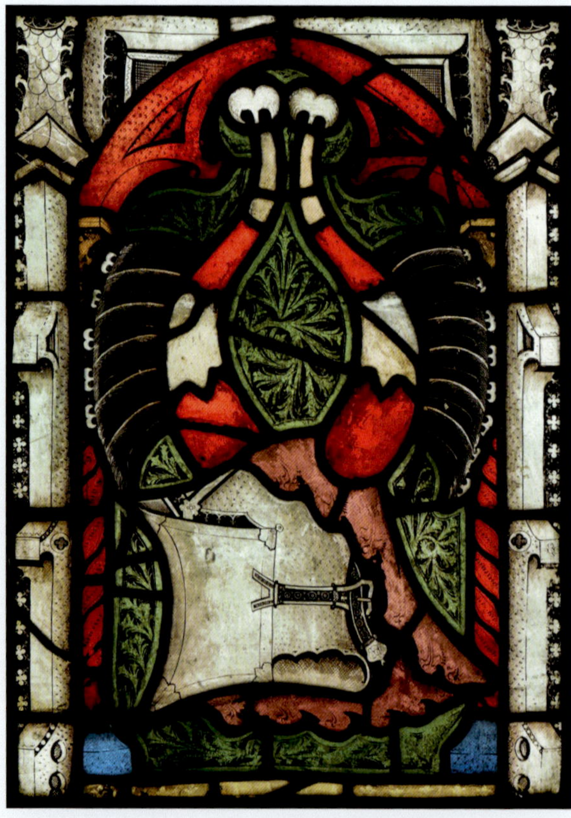

This panel is one of the two ornate helms with crests
within the series. This example depicts a jousting helm
fitted with a 'wrapper', a reinforcing plate strapped
and buckled to the front of the helm. (45.486.1.b)

The 12 panels may represent remnants of multiple windows, although their unform style and dimensions imply a shared provenance. Linguistic and stylistic evidence suggests the glass was made in northern Germany, possibly in or near the Hanseatic town of Lüneburg, Lower Saxony. The architectural canopies are reminiscent of those found in the cloister windows of the former Benedictine convent at Ebstorf. The Burrell panels may have originated from the same workshop and can be similarly dated to the end of the fourteenth or early fifteenth century.

Such pieces made at Lüneburg or Lower Saxony are rarely encountered outside of Germany, with no other windows from this region recorded in collections in the UK or USA.

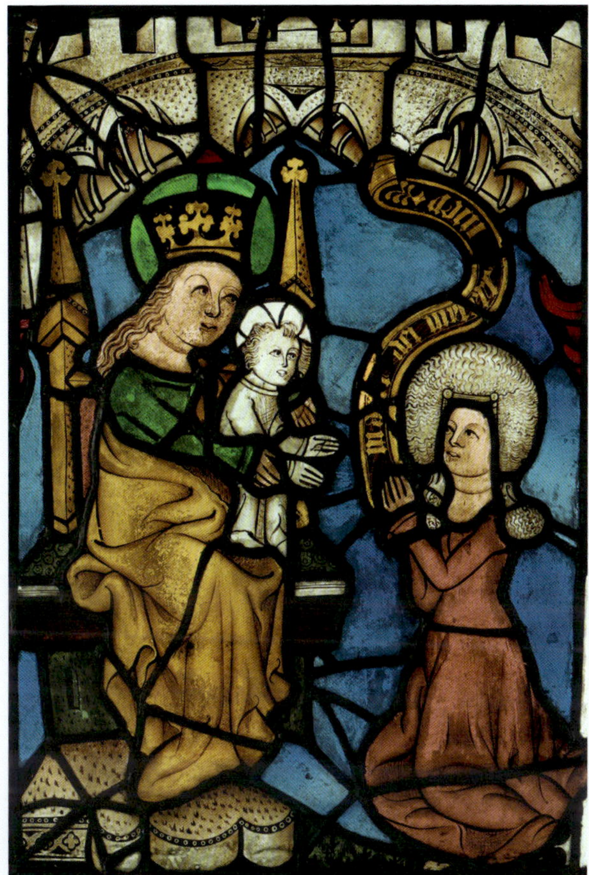

Dating evidence is provided via this female donor's distinctive headwear. The frilled '*kruseler*' head-dress, with distinctive pom-pom endings, supports a probable date of execution in the late 1300s to early 1400s.

(45.486.6.a)

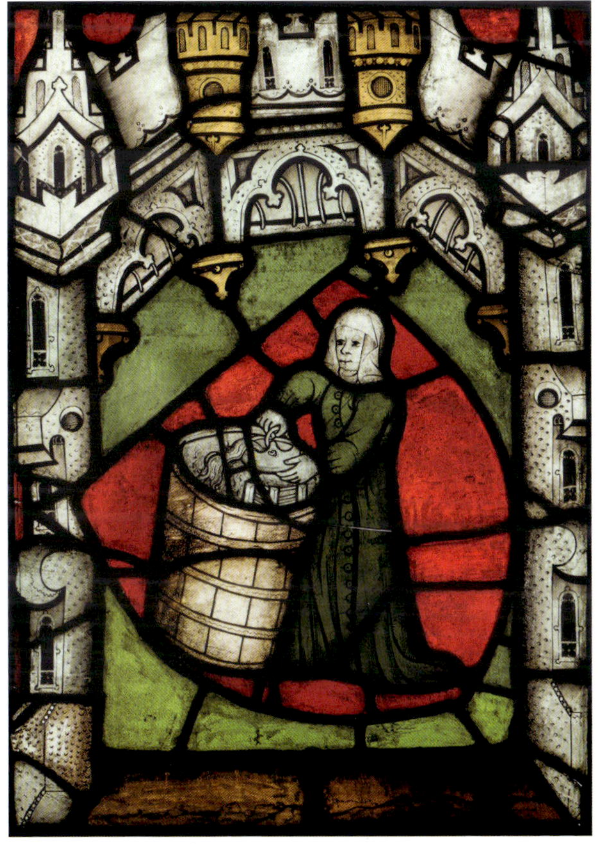

Left: With their detailed representations of wool-washing and dyeing, shield-making, and agricultural work, it seems likely that these 12 panels originated somewhere with both a sizeable urban population and a close relationship to the countryside.

(45.486.1.a)

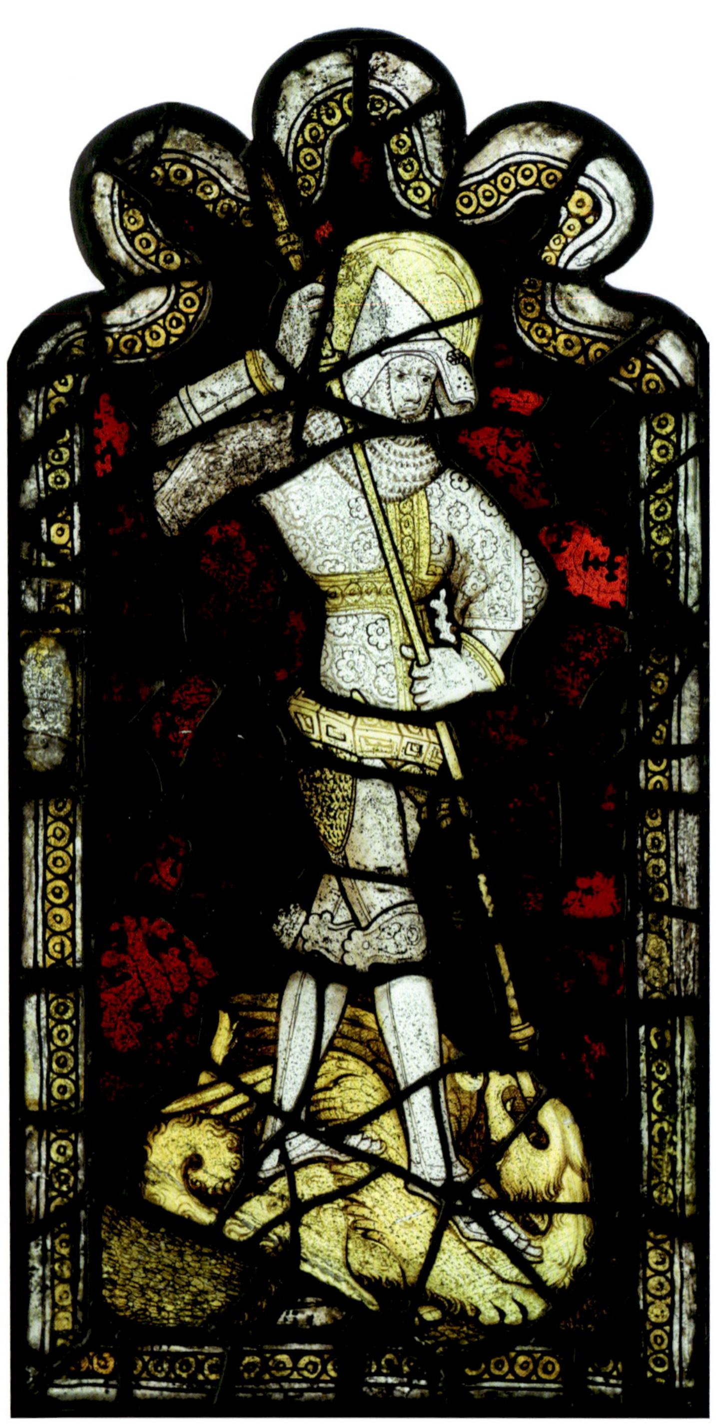

St George and the Dragon,
about 1400
Made in England
Colourless glass, pot metal glass,
vitreous paint, silver stain, lead
70 cm x 34.5 cm x 1 cm
45.86

By tradition St George was born in the
province of Cappadocia in modern-day
Turkey. Despite serving in the Roman
military, he was martyred for his faith during
the Roman persecution of Christians in
303 AD. Originating in the east, St George's
cult was popularized in western Europe
via his inclusion in Jacobus de Voragine's
(d.1298) widely circulated and influential
compendium of saints' lives, *The Golden
Legend*.

St George is shown slaying a dragon
pinned beneath his feet. His arms and
armour help date the panel to around
1400. Details such as the pointed *bascinet*
(helmet) fitted with a protective mail
aventail (a mail curtain covering the neck
and shoulders), would have been familiar
to the warrior-saint's devotees amongst
the martial knightly classes of late
medieval Europe.

St Stephen, about 1400–20
Made in Styria, Austria
Colourless glass, pot metal glass,
vitreous paint, silver stain, lead
79.5 cm x 36.8 cm x 1 cm
45.383

Probably of Greek Jewish origin, according
to the New Testament's Act of the Apostles
(Acts 6-8), St Stephen was one of first
deacons of the emerging Christian Church.
Accused of blasphemy and put on trial
by the Jewish authorities, St Stephen's
passionate defence of Christianity so
inflamed the crowd that he was stoned
to death.

Regarded as the first Christian martyr,
Stephen stands in a graceful and serene
stance, cradling the stones of his execution,
and holding a palm leaf, symbolic of the
triumph of faith over the suffering of the
martyr's death. The panel's bold linear
painting style and use of brilliant colour
is typical of Austrian glass of this period.

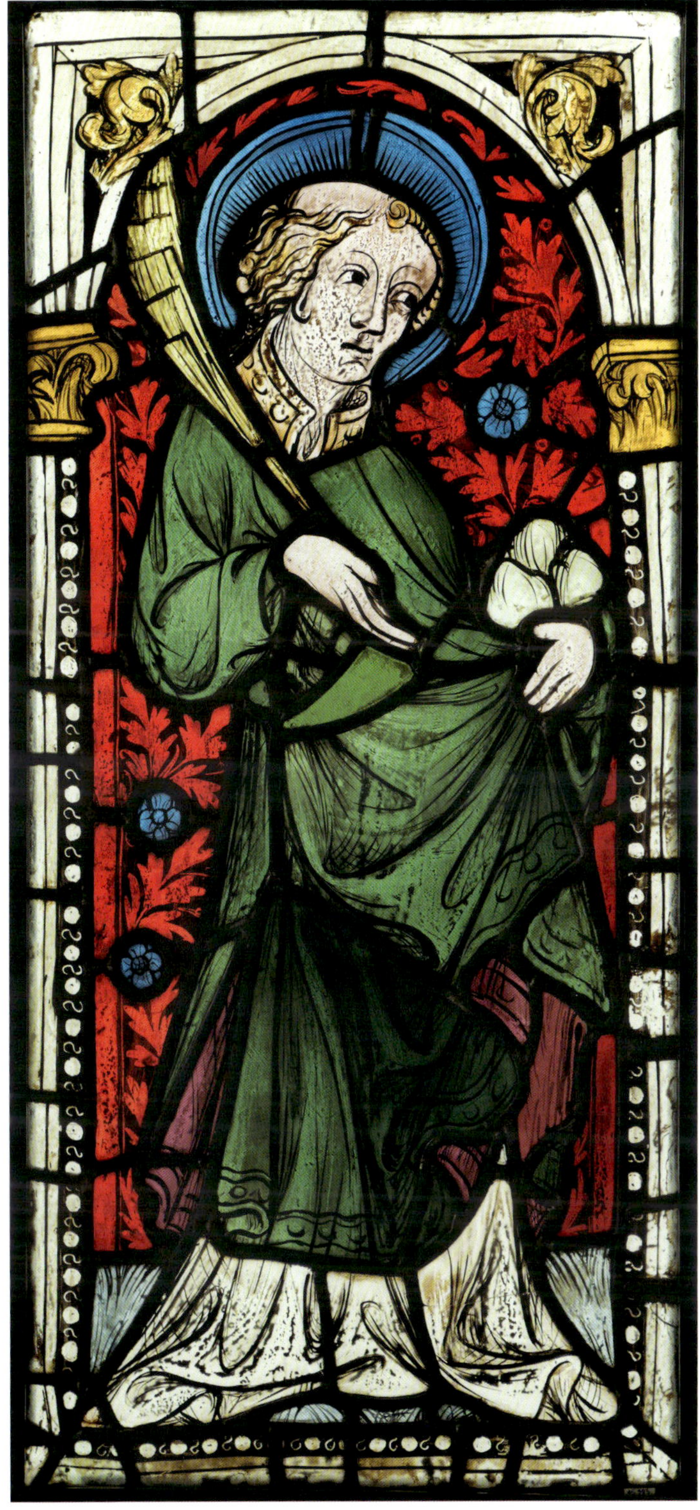

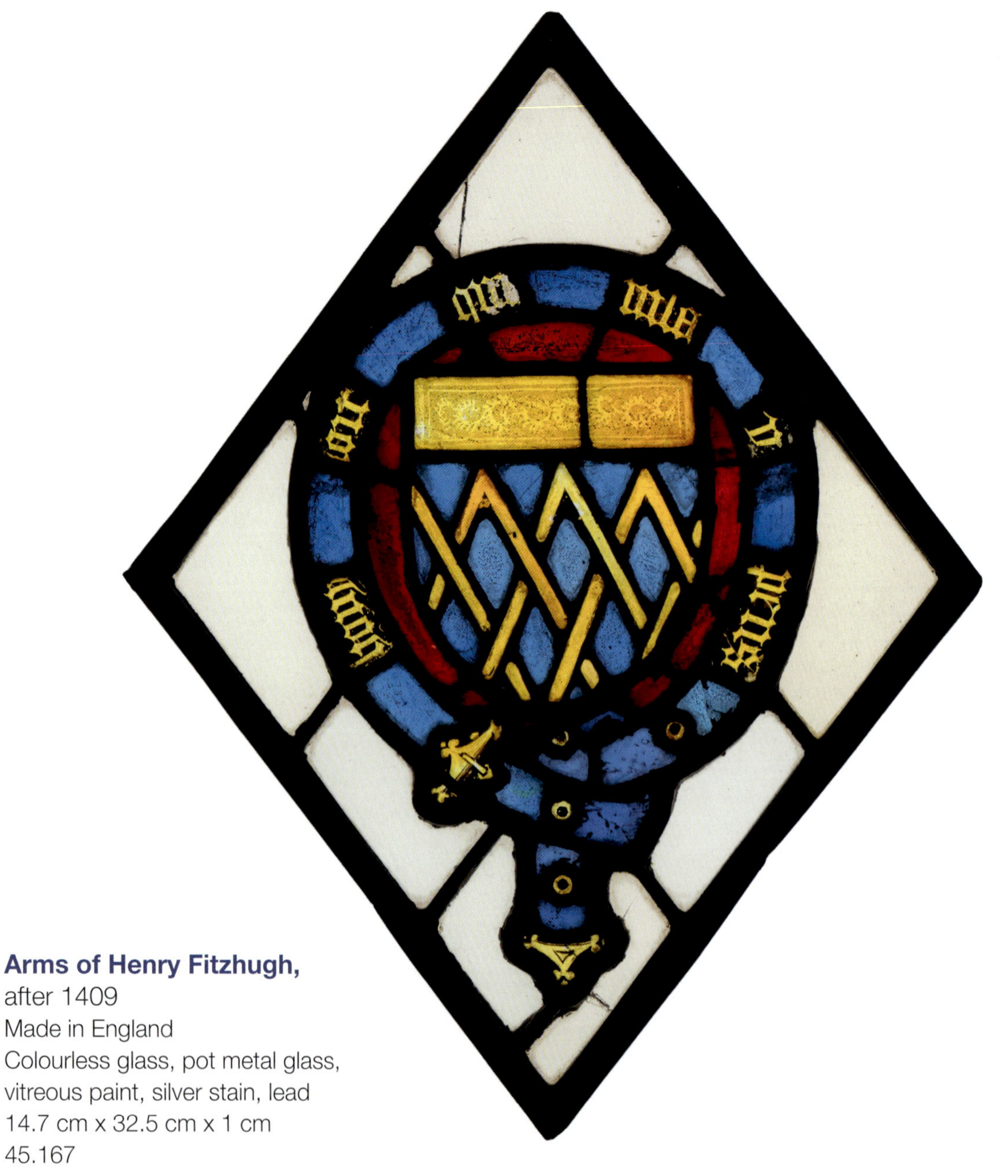

Arms of Henry Fitzhugh,
after 1409
Made in England
Colourless glass, pot metal glass,
vitreous paint, silver stain, lead
14.7 cm x 32.5 cm x 1 cm
45.167

Founded by King Edward III in 1348, the Most Noble Order of the Garter is amongst Europe's oldest chivalric orders and the most senior order of chivalry in medieval England. The men elected to its ranks commissioned heraldic stained glass incorporating the Order's insignia as a means of celebrating and commemorating the honour bestowed upon them. Henry Fitzhugh, 3rd Baron Fitzhugh (about 1363–1425) was appointed as Knight of the Garter in 1409. He held several administrative roles and participated in military and diplomatic engagements for King Henry IV (1367–1413) and his son, King Henry V (1386–1422). This medallion is reputed to be the oldest surviving stained glass to include the Order's motto and garter device.

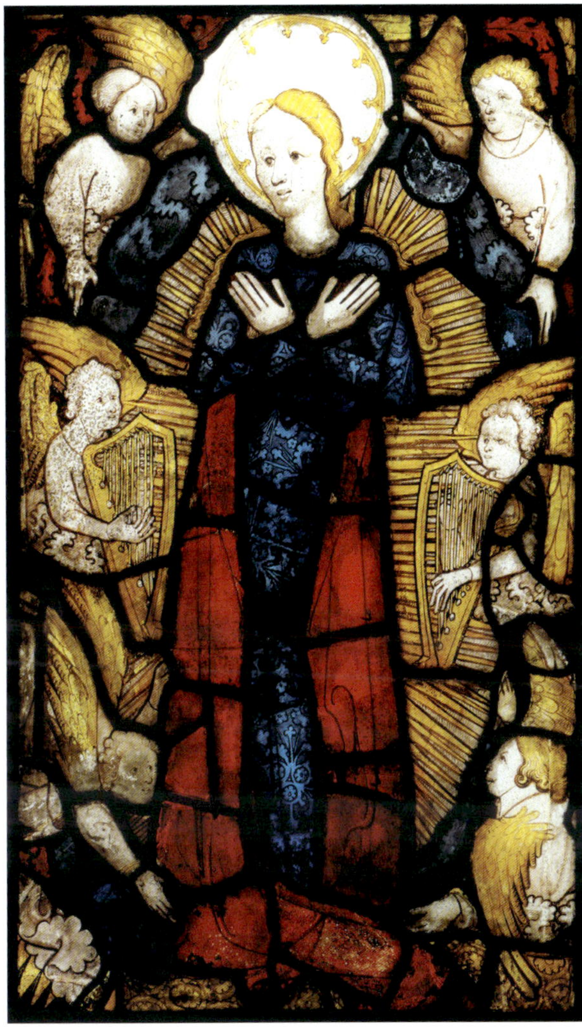

Annunciation and Assumption of the Virgin,
about 1420–35
Made in England, possibly from the Workshop of
John Thornton
Colourless glass, pot metal glass, vitreous paint,
silver stain, lead
81 cm x 48.9 m x 1 cm
80.5 cm x 48 cm x 1 cm
From the chapel of Hampton Court Castle,
Herefordshire, England
45.588, 45.589

Acquired by the Burrell Trustees in 1979, these two
panels came from the chapel of Hampton Court
Castle, Herefordshire. Assumed to have been built
by Sir Rowland Lenthall (d.1450), the chapel was
once home to several stained glass panels, including
examples now in the Victoria and Albert Museum,
London, and the Museum of Fine Arts, Boston.

Although these surviving panels date to around the
time of the chapel's supposed construction, signs of
alteration to some of them implies that they may have
originated elsewhere – possibly Hereford Cathedral.

Stylistic parallels have been drawn between the
chapel windows and the work of the celebrated
glazier John Thornton of Coventry (fl. 1405–33),
whose workshop produced some of fifteenth-century
England's finest stained glass windows.

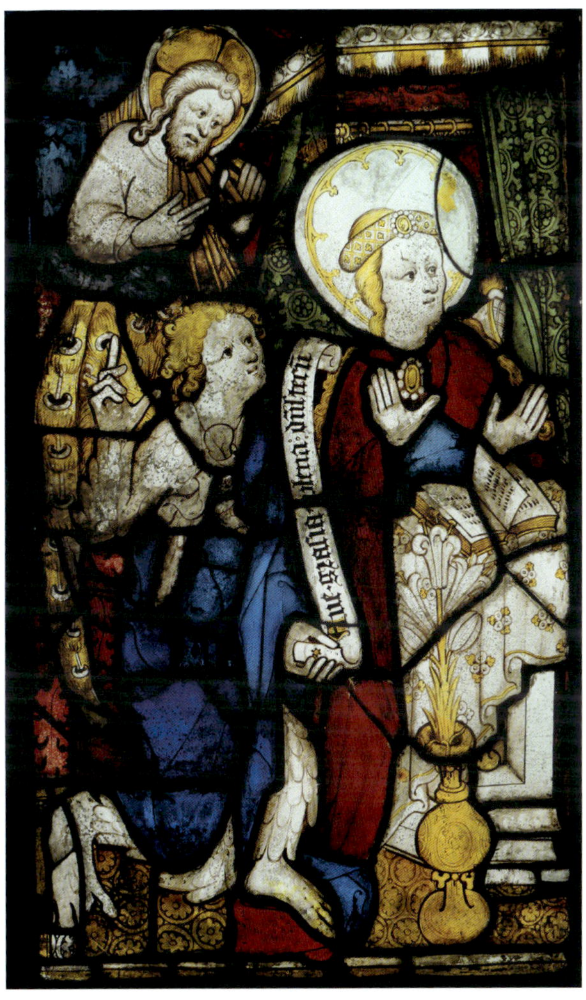

Objects in Focus

Six windows showing the Life of Jesus Christ and the Virgin Mary, 1444

Made in the Upper Rhine, Germany
Colourless glass, pot metal glass, vitreous paint, silver stain, lead
260 cm x 230 cm x 1 cm
Removed from the Carmelite Church of Boppard-am-Rhein, Germany
45.485

These monumental panels once formed part of a much larger 'Tree of Jesse' window (see p.62), in which the genealogy of Christ was replaced by scenes from the Life of Christ and the Virgin. They are from the former Carmelite Church of Boppard-am-Rhein. As patroness of the Carmelites, Mary is given unusual prominence in the window, with her Nativity and the Annunciation at the centre of the composition. The window was one of seven commissioned for the glazing programme of the new north nave of the monastery, consecrated at Boppard in 1444.

Secularized by Napoleon during the French occupation of the Rhineland (1794–1814), the monastery at Boppard was disbanded, and the building handed over to the care of the town officials. Greatly impoverished by the events of recent years, the town could afford neither the repair nor the maintenance of the windows, and sold the entire cycle to a German aristocrat, Count Hermann von Pückler-Muskau (1785–1871), in 1818.

The Boppard glass is now widely dispersed but several important panels were acquired by Burrell in the late 1930s. These particular windows were purchased in 1938 from William Randolph Hearst (see also pp.13, 17, 24 and 34). They are some of Burrell's most expensive stained glass acquisitions. While he bemoaned paying what he regarded as

'very full prices' for the Hearst glass, it was these additions that prompted Wilfred Drake to justifiably remark that Burrell was now the owner of 'the finest private collection [of stained glass] in existence.'

The windows show Christ before Pilate and the Agony in the Garden (left), the Annunciation, the Nativity of Mary (centre), the Resurrection of Christ and Christ appearing to Peter (right).

An appreciation of the original glazing scheme of the church's north nave is today possible through the recent efforts of the Boppard Traffic and Beautification Association (*Verkehrs- und Verschönerungs-Verein Boppard*). The Association has used high resolution images of the dispersed windows from various institutions, including the Burrell Collection, the Met Cloisters in New York, and the Museum-Schnütgen in Cologne. Spectacular full-scale replicas printed on fabric banners overlay the now clear glazing, providing a vivid and moving impression of the church's late medieval character.

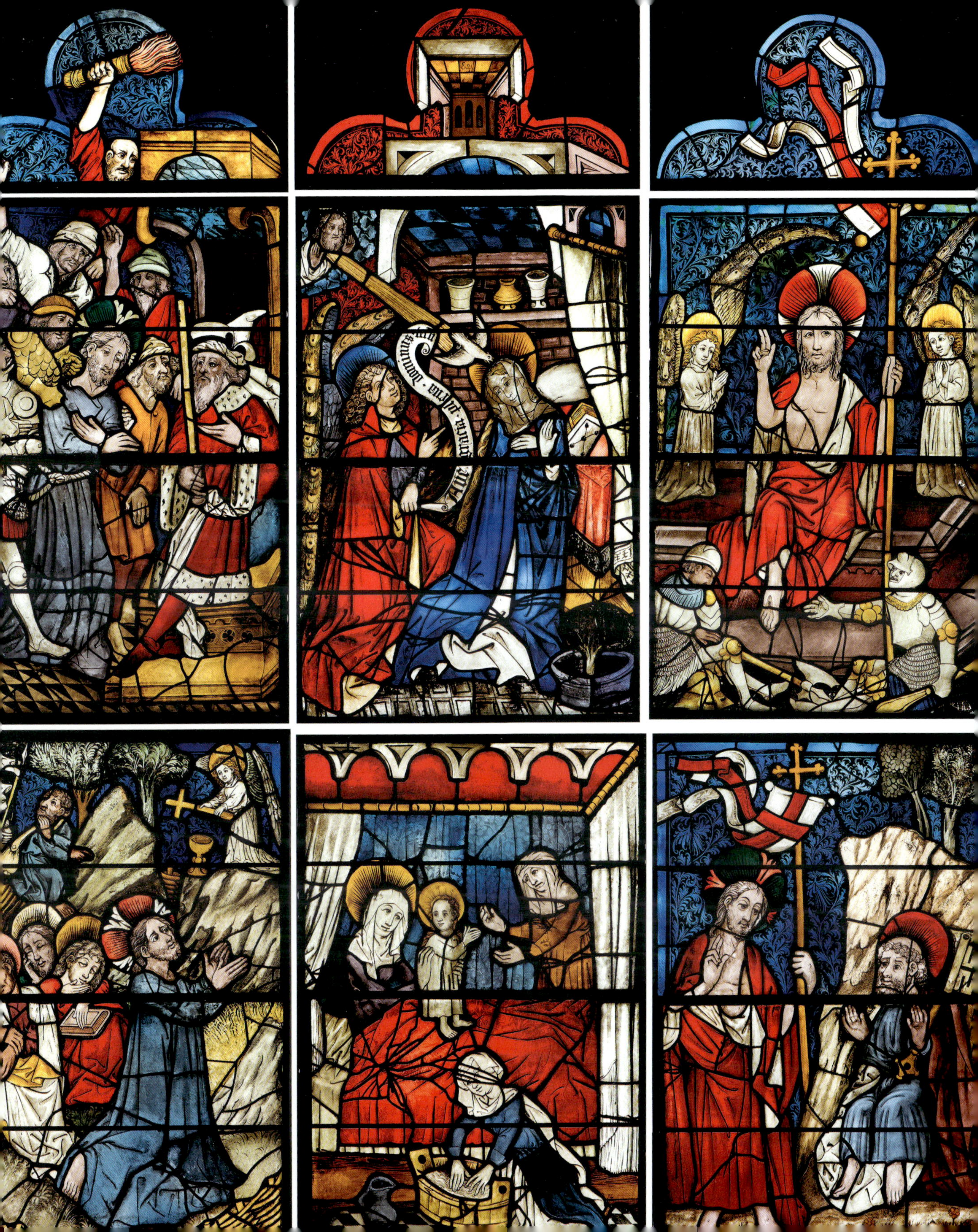

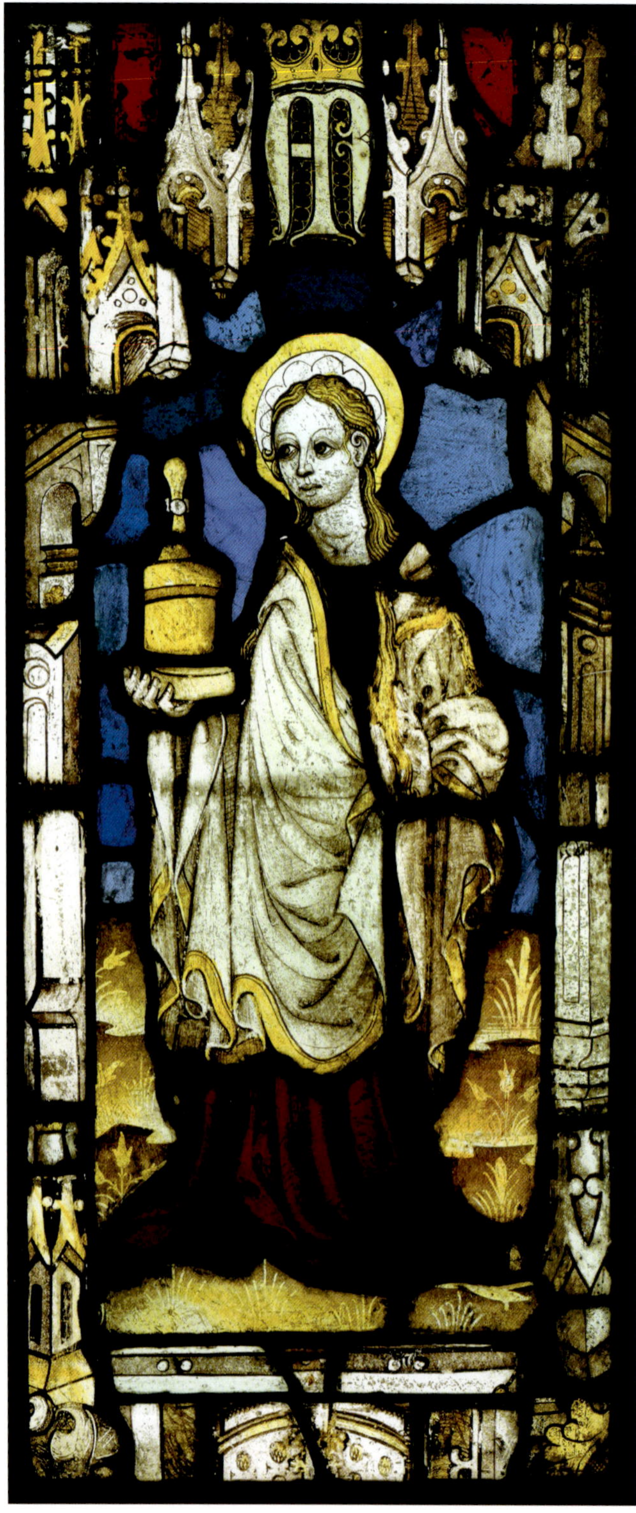

St Mary Magdalene?, about 1445–55

Made in Norwich, England
Colourless glass, pot metal glass,
vitreous paint, silver stain, lead
62 cm x 26.5 cm x 1 cm
45.37

This arrangement corresponds closely with that of another female saint, possibly St Barbara, now in the Metropolitan Museum of Art, New York. Sharing the same dimensions, pose, and extravagant drapery, the figures, which undoubtedly derive from the same cartoon, are reversed and further distinguished by alterations to the attributes they hold.

Identification of the Burrell figure is complicated by later additions; neither the crowned 'M', associated with the Virgin Mary, nor the ointment jar, which is conventionally attributed to Mary Magdalene, is original. Both panels may have come from a series devoted to female saints, of which several comparable examples survive in the upper tracery lights of Norfolk church windows, including St Margaret's Church, Cley-next-the-Sea.

St John the Evangelist Hands the Palm to the Jewish Chief Priest, 1450–55

Made in Norwich, England, attributed to the workshop of John Wighton
Colourless glass, pot metal glass, vitreous paint, silver stain, lead
67.9 cm x 48.3 cm x 1 cm
From the 'Toppes' window, the Church of St Peter Mancroft, Norwich, England
45.92

The finely modelled figures of this panel, with their lively expressions and tightly curled hair, are characteristic of the Norwich School of glass painting, and can be attributed to the workshop of John Wighton (d.1457). Norwich grew prosperous through the wool trade, and by the fifteenth century it was England's second largest city, able to sustain a flourishing stained glass industry.

This panel, depicting the apocryphal conversion of a Jewish priest following his failed attempt to disrupt the funeral of the Virgin Mary, comes from the Toppes window of St Peter Mancroft Church, Norwich. A large multi-panel arrangement dedicated to the Virgin, the Toppes window was commissioned by Robert Toppes (d.1467), a merchant and four-time Mayor of Norwich.

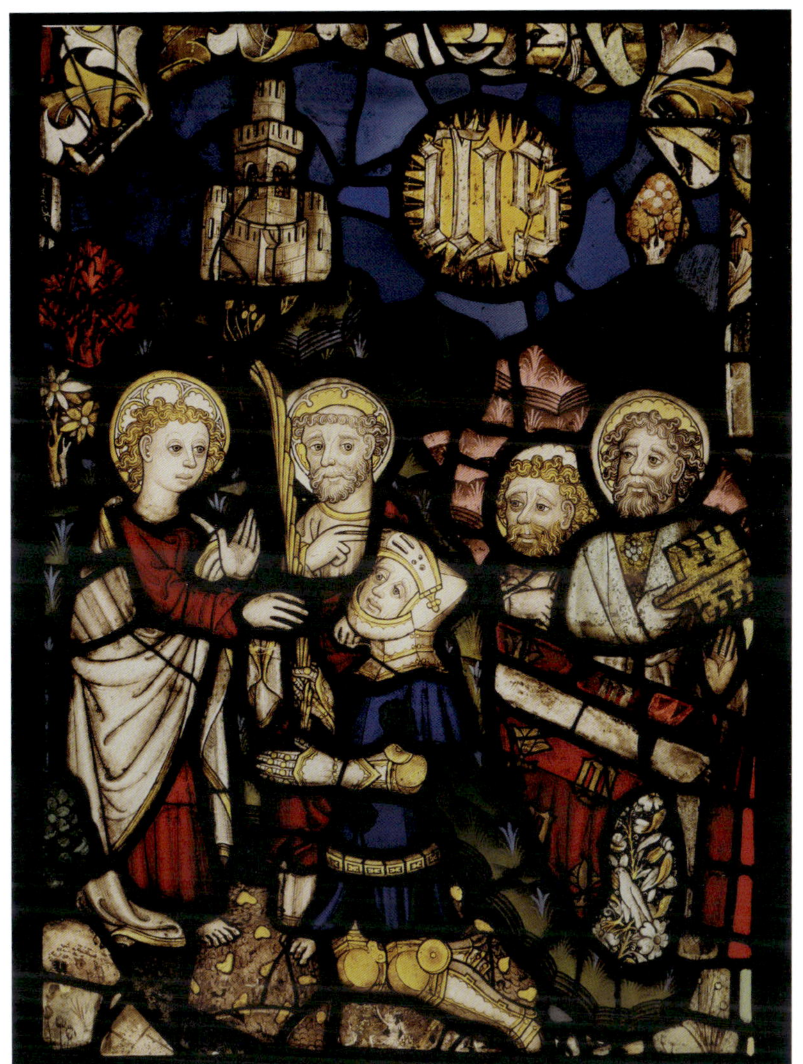

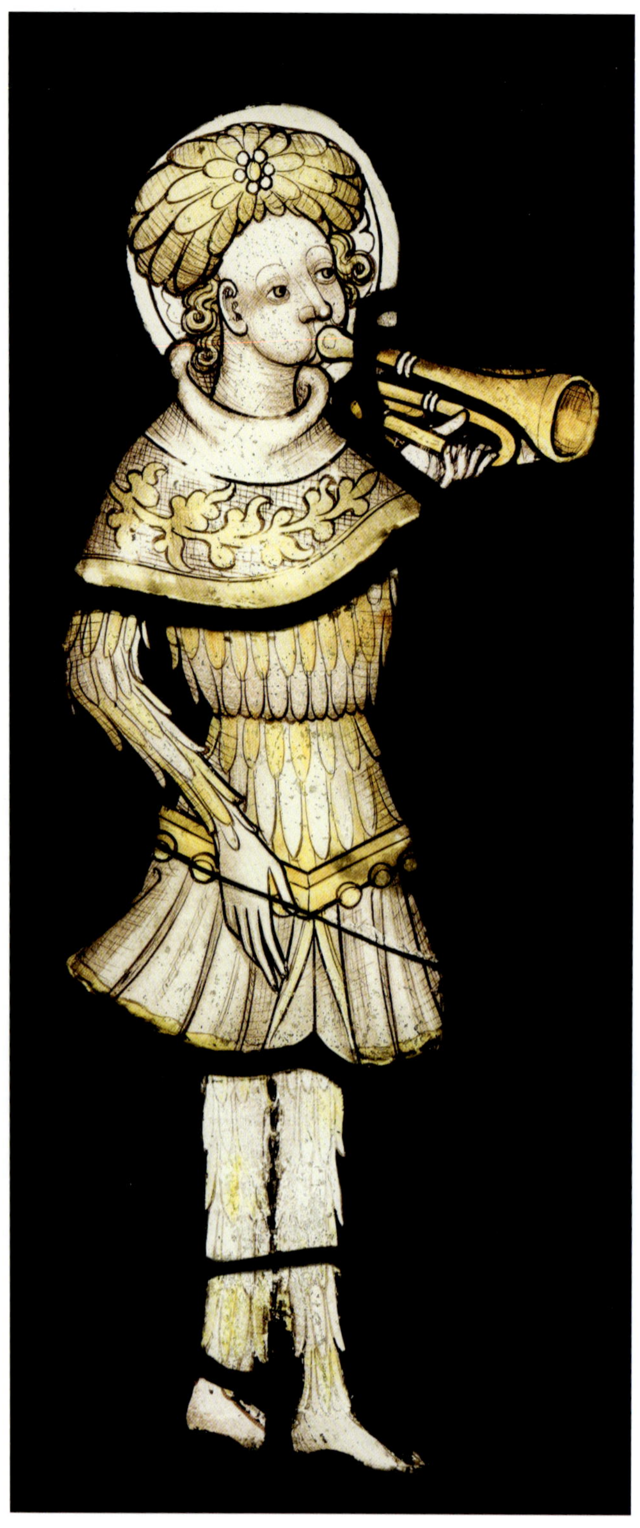

Bugle-playing Angel, about 1460–80
Made in Norwich, England
Colourless glass, vitreous paint, silver stain, lead
41.5 cm x 19.5 cm x 1 m
45.84

Angels were a common feature of fifteenth-century English church glazing. Frequently encountered in the carved tracery openings at the summit of large multi-light windows, angels sometimes hold scrolls containing religious verse, grasp liturgical items, or play musical instruments.

Musical angels were particularly prominent in medieval stained glass, as evidenced in Norfolk churches, where angelic orchestras sometimes accompanied holy scenes such as the Annunciation, or the Coronation of the Virgin as the Queen of Heaven. This angel's feathered suit and bell-strung belt were perhaps inspired by the costumes worn by actors in medieval religious drama performances known as 'mystery plays'.

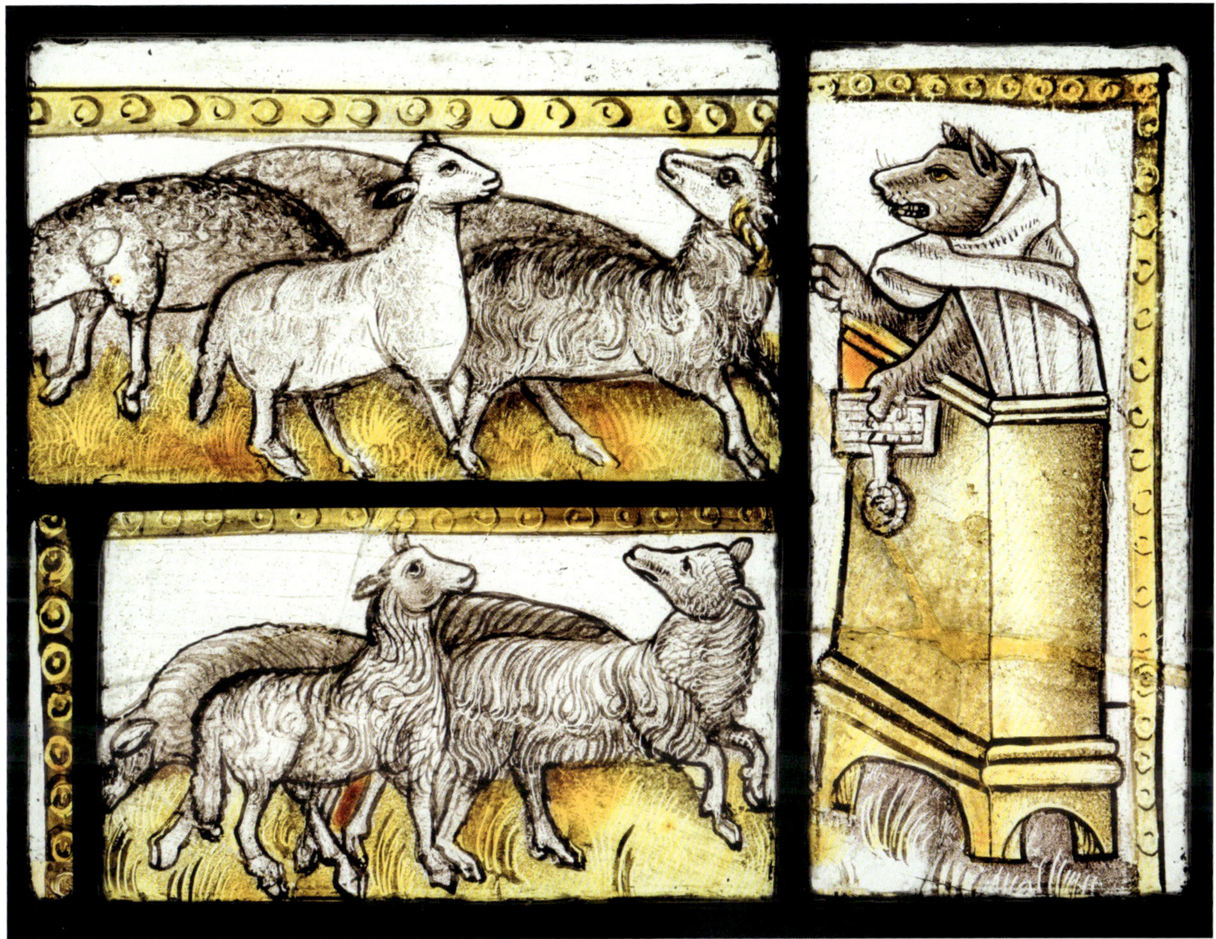

Wolf Preaching to Sheep, 1400–1500

Made in England

Colourless glass, vitreous paint, silver stain, lead

18.5 cm x 24.6 cm x 1 cm

45.64

In an act of cunning deception, a wolf dressed as a cleric preaches to a flock of sheep from the pulpit, enticing his gullible prey closer with his false words.

Imagery of the duplicitous preaching fox or wolf was utilized by both defenders of the Catholic Church and its reformist critics as a humorous metaphor for their opponents' false preaching, corruption, and deceit. The document brandished by the wolf perhaps represents an indulgence; a grant sold by the Church to the faithful, promising a remission from punishment after death. Many reformers opposed the practice, regarding the granting of indulgences as an unscrupulous commercial act.

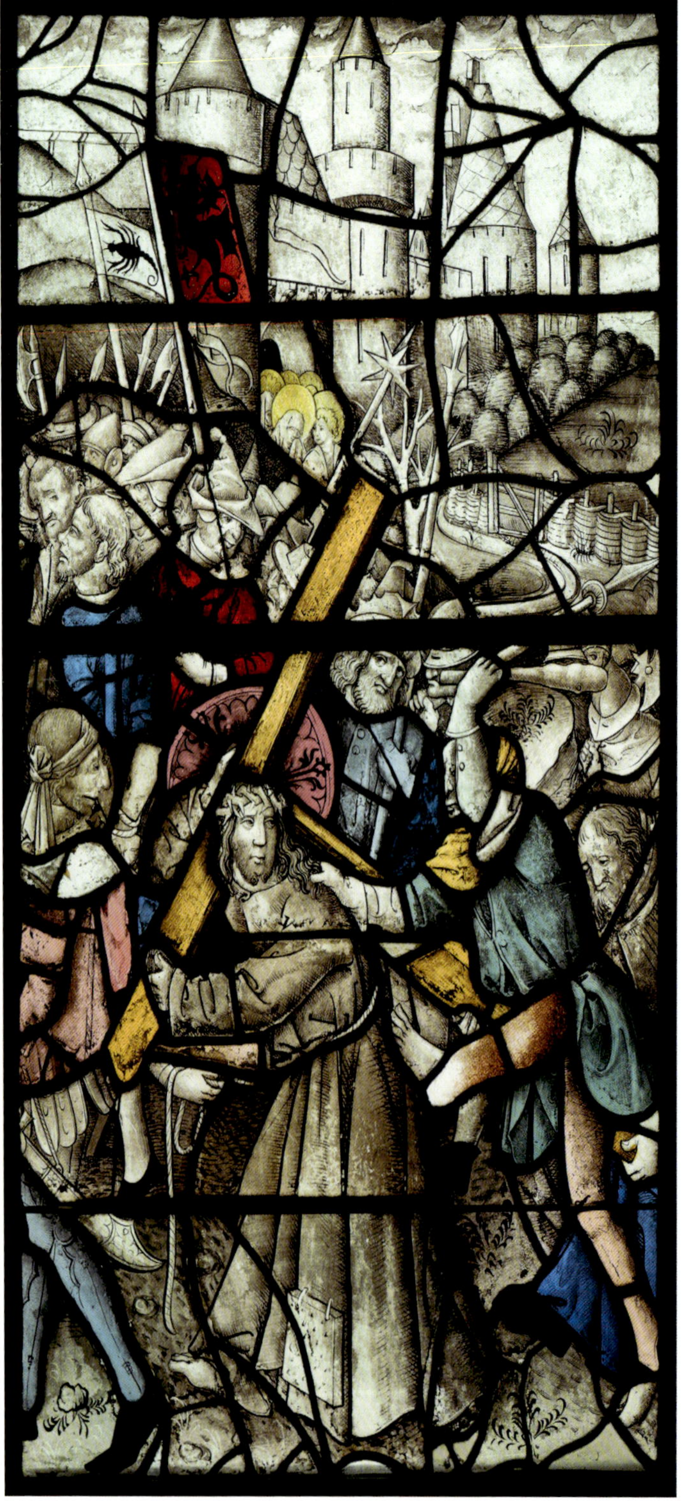

Christ Carrying the Cross, about 1465
Made in Cologne, Germany, attributed to the
St Cecilia workshop
Colourless glass, pot metal glass, vitreous paint,
silver stain, lead
Overall: 104.8 cm x 58.4 mm x 1 cm
45.431

This panel depicts the Carrying of the Cross
and is thought to be the product of the prolific
St Cecilia workshop, so-named after stained
glass it is understood to have produced for the
church of St Cecilia in Cologne. It was once
part of a larger cycle dedicated to the Passion
of Christ. Cologne was a major centre for
producing stained glass. Its late medieval glaziers
streamlined their production by repeating scenes
and reusing cartoons, which by this time were
increasingly drawn on paper. Two other almost
identical versions of this panel are known: one
at St Nicolas Church, Great Bookham, Surrey,
England, and another at Cologne Cathedral,
Germany.

As is characteristic of Cologne glass of this
period, the panel displays a restrained use
of eye-drawing colour, relying on clear glass
painted with great clarity and legibility.

King Solomon receives the Queen of Sheba, about 1460–80

Made in Cologne, Germany
Colourless glass, pot metal glass,
vitreous paint, silver stain, lead
80.3 cm x 57.5 cm x 1 cm
45.432

Medieval art typically mirrors the fashions and customs of its own time. Drawing inspiration from their everyday lives, medieval artists transported historical and biblical events into a world resembling their own. In doing so, they produced works that resonated with, and were familiar to, their contemporary audiences.

Despite the ancient source material, this panel depicting the meeting of the biblical King Solomon and the Queen of Sheba (1 Kings 10:2) provides invaluable insight into late medieval dress. The ermine trimmed cloth of gold, elaborate headwear, and the attendant's short tunic, hose or stockings, and extravagantly pointed shoes (*poulaines*), reflect the luxurious and ostentatious fashions of the fifteenth-century court.

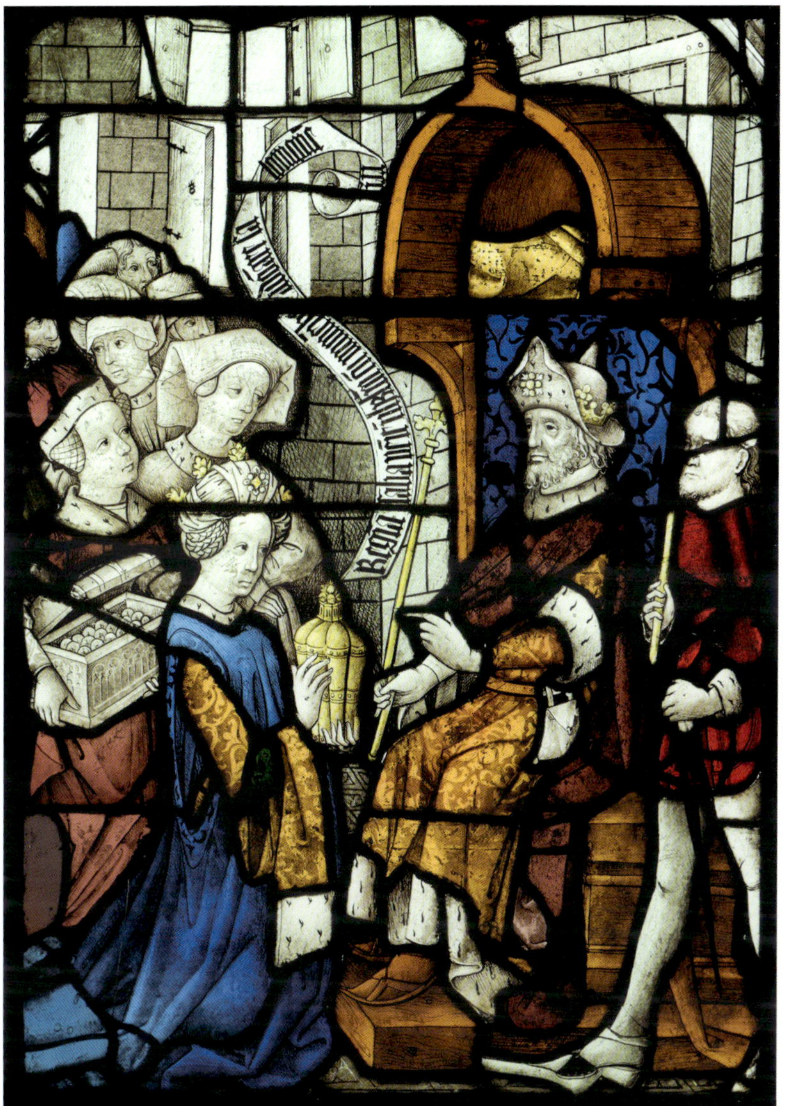

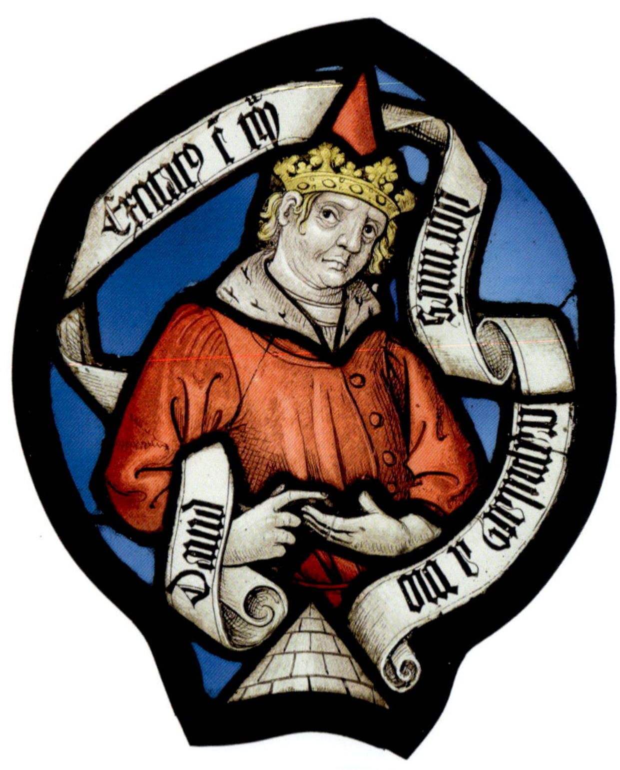

King David and Zechariah, about 1470
Probably made by the St Cecilia workshop,
Cologne, Germany
Colourless glass, pot metal glass, vitreous paint,
silver stain, lead
35.8 cm x 30 cm x 1 cm
34 cm x 29 cm x 1 cm
45.385, 45.386

These portraits, depicting the Old Testament's King
David and the prophet Zechariah, almost certainly
belonged to a typological series juxtaposing events
and verses of the Old and New Testaments (see p.14).
In the fifteenth century, models for such windows
were provided by contemporary printed texts known
as *Biblia Pauperum* (Paupers' Bible); popular picture
books relaying the key stories and messages of the
Christian faith.

Several museums hold stylistically similar pieces,
all attributed to the St Cecilia workshop of Cologne.
These panels may have originally formed part of a
cycle in which Old Testament figures were placed in
the upper traceried parts of the window, set above
larger narrative scenes.

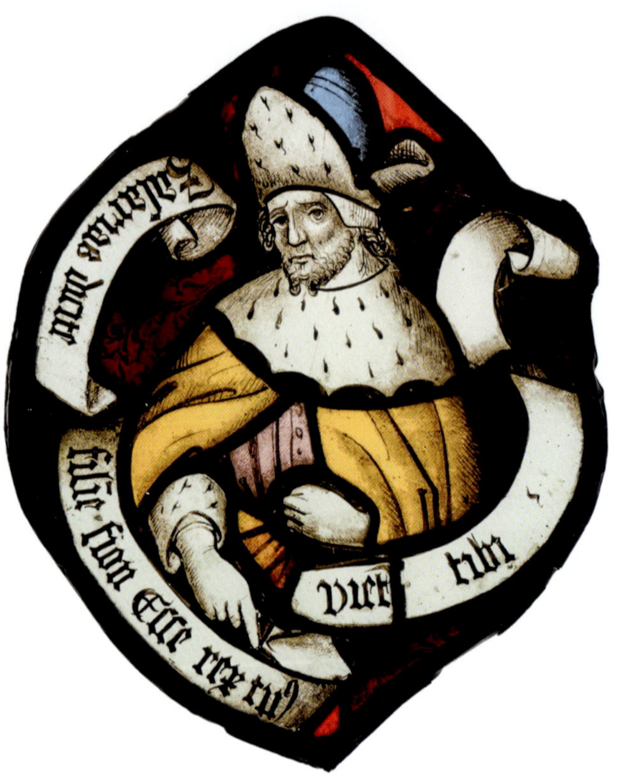

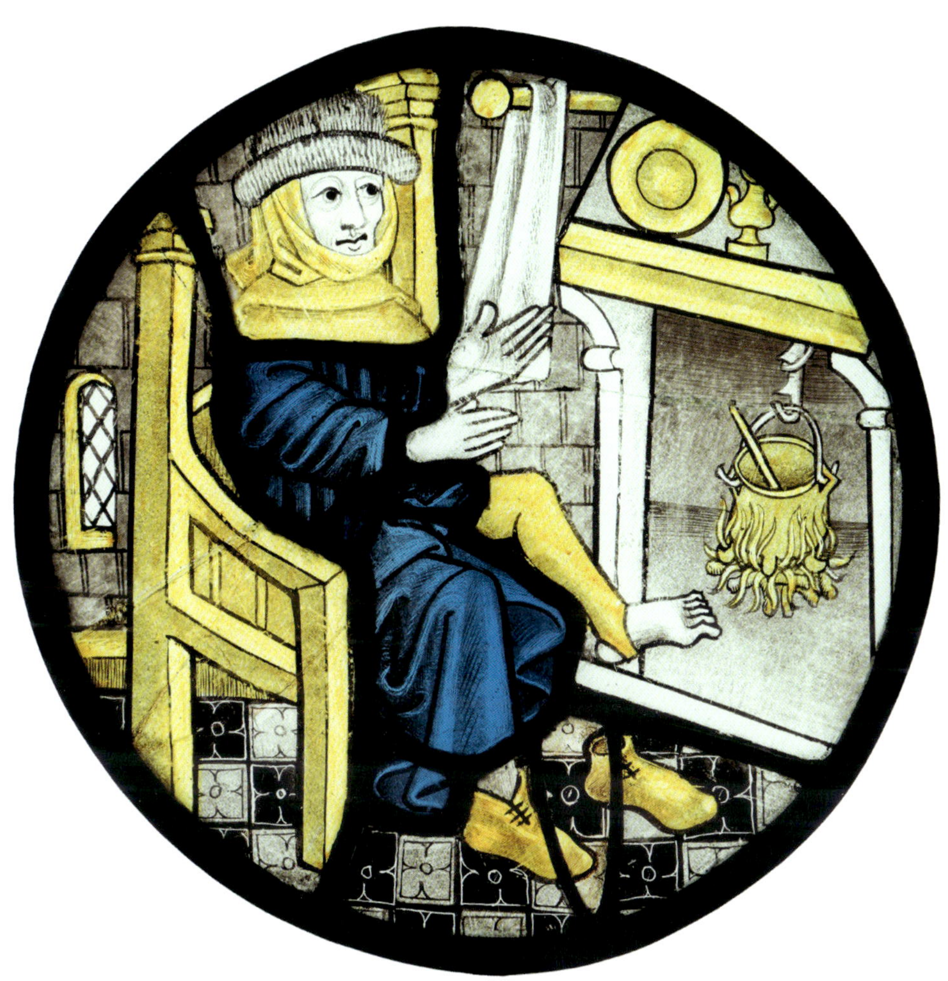

Labour of the Month; probably February,
about 1480

Made in Norfolk, England
Colourless glass, pot metal glass, vitreous paint, silver stain, lead
24.2 cm x 24.2 cm x 1 cm
Possibly from St Michael-at-Coslany, Norwich, England
45.83

Wrapped up against the cold, a man in a fur hat and blue robe warms himself by the hearth as a cauldron hangs over a roaring fire. This fascinating and relatable scene of domestic comfort probably represents February and relates to a larger 12-roundel cycle dedicated to the Labours of the Months. This was a popular theme found throughout medieval art. Such series offer charming insight into late medieval rural life and society through their interpretations of seasonal activities and agricultural customs.

These windows are said to be from the same set as three roundels in the Victoria and Albert Museum, London, formerly installed in the old parsonage at St Michael-at-Coslany, Norwich.

Object in Focus

Princess Cecily of York, 1483–84
Made in England
Colourless glass, pot metal glass, vitreous paint,
silver stain, lead
40 cm x 30.5 cm x 1 cm
Removed from the 'Royal' window of Canterbury
Cathedral, Kent, England
45.75

One of the Burrell Collection's most celebrated stained glass panels, this portrait, identified as Princess Cecily of York (1469–1507), once formed part of the 'Royal' window erected in the north-west transept of Canterbury Cathedral, Kent.

In 1643 the window was badly damaged by the zealous Puritan minister and iconoclast Richard Culmer (1597–1662). An impression of the window's original design is provided by the modern reconstruction now seen at Canterbury. There, Cecily, and six siblings, including Edward, Prince of Wales (later Edward V) (1470–83), are presented kneeling in prayer either side of their parents, King Edward IV (1442–83) and Elizabeth Woodville (about 1437–92).

The Cecily panel, most likely a royal commission, represents some of the most technically and artistically accomplished English glass of the period. Reminiscent of contemporary Netherlandish panel painting, the window's realistic portraiture has drawn comparison with the paintings of Ghent's Hugo van der Goes (1440–82) and may be the work of highly skilled immigrant craftsmen.

Corresponding with Burrell shortly after this panel was purchased in 1939, dealer Wilfred Drake remarked that he hoped Cecily would one day serve as a companion piece to Sir William's earlier royal portrait of Beatrix of Valkenburg (p.16), describing them both as 'fine example[s]… full of Romantic interest'.

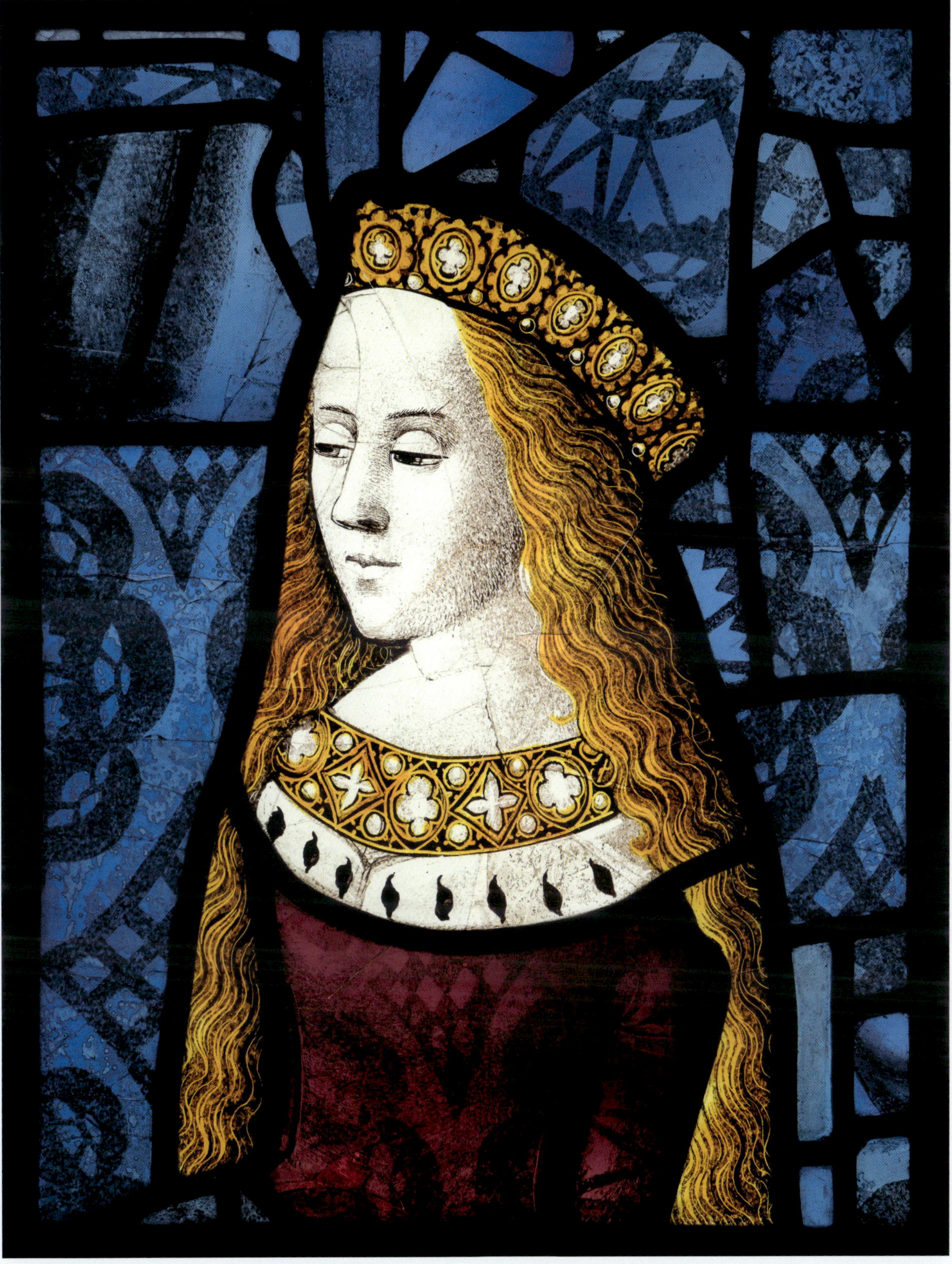

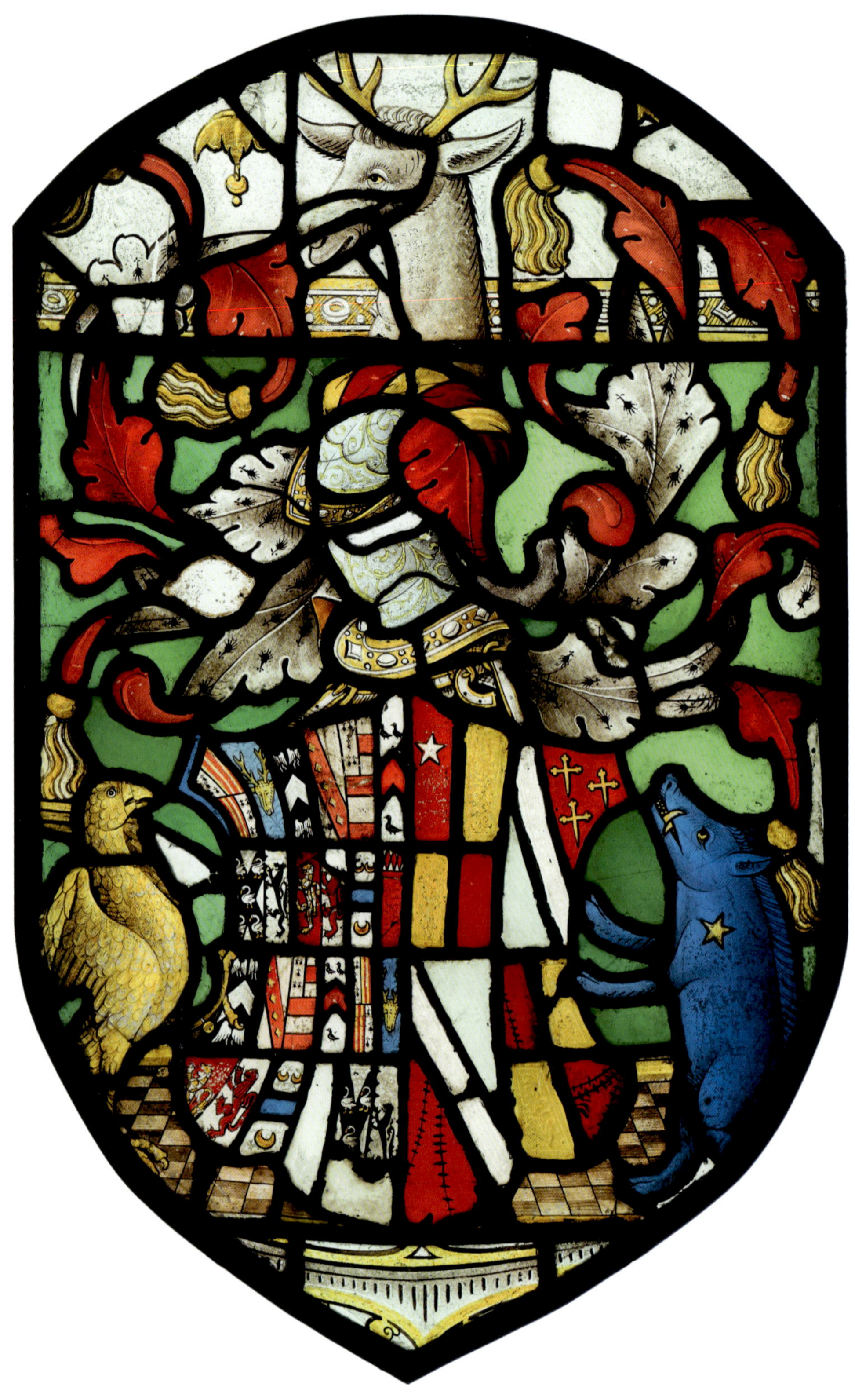

Sixteenth-century Glass

At the beginning of the sixteenth century the stained glass industry continued to thrive. The influence of Netherlandish art and the wider Renaissance aesthetic, with its greater appreciation of perspective, realistic portraiture and landscapes, persisted and took even greater hold. Aided not least by the wider circulation of contemporary prints, glass painters became increasingly familiar with the work of Europe's leading artists, some of whom, such as Germany's Albrecht Dürer (1471–1528), produced their own stained glass designs. Netherlandish glass painters were particularly sought after for their expertise and refined painterly skills. They travelled throughout Europe on lucrative commissions, entering the service of rich and powerful patrons.

However, as the century progressed the fortunes of glass painters deteriorated significantly as a consequence of the religious reformations that swept through much of northern Europe. Regarded as idolatrous and superstitious, stained glass was violently stripped from religious houses in waves of iconoclastic destruction. Deprived of new ecclesiastical commissions, glass painters turned much of their creative energies towards secular and heraldic glass, producing small-scale and armorial works for churches, civic spaces, and private homes.

In the middle of the century, innovations in colouring techniques brought great and lasting change to the art of stained glass. With the development of coloured vitreous enamel paints, the glass painter was able to paint and fire colour directly onto glass in a manner akin to painting on a panel or canvas. As a result, traditionally coloured pot metal glass and lead-lines became less integral to stained glass arrangement and design.

It was in the 1930s, with Burrell approaching his late seventies, that Constance and he decided to donate their remarkable art collection to public ownership, eventually agreeing upon Glasgow as the recipient in 1944. No longer constrained by the confines of Hutton Castle, from the mid-1930s onwards Burrell greatly expanded and enhanced his collection, acquiring some of his finest treasures for the benefit of the future museum that would one day bear his name.

Burrell's most expensive pieces were bought during these years, with some of the largest and costliest stained glass obtained from the noted American collector and newspaper publisher William Randolph Hearst in 1938–39 (see p.39). Hearst's own collecting was curtailed by near financial collapse in 1937, and the market amongst private collectors was generally less competitive than it had been prior to the financial recession initiated by the Great Crash in 1929. Having avoided the financial difficulties suffered by others, and outliving many of his erstwhile competitors, latterly Burrell was vying alongside museums for the very best glass on the market.

Opposite: Over a quarter of the stained glass collection takes the form of English armorials. Burrell greatly admired English heraldic glass, stating that 'It has not only colour, but… being armorial is intensely interesting'. (Detail of 45.332, see p.71)

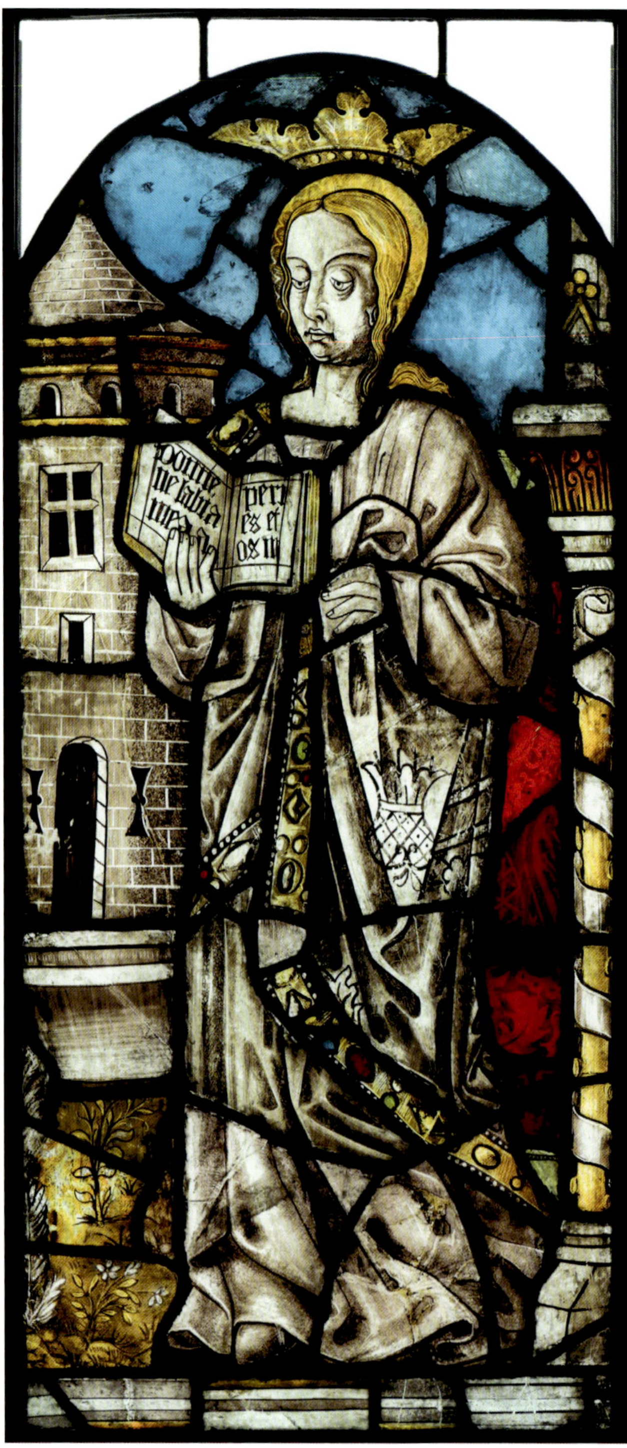

St Barbara, about 1500

Made in France or Germany
Colourless glass, pot metal glass, vitreous paint,
silver stain, lead
106 cm x 47 cm x 1 cm
45.403

Standing in a garden before the tower in which she
was said to have been imprisoned by her pagan
father, St Barbara holds open a book carrying the
words of Psalm 51:15, '*Domine labia mea aperies
et os m[eum]*', translated as 'Lord, you will open my
lips and my mouth'.

This panel retains rare vestiges of ornamentation;
jewel-like additions of coloured glass, imitating
rubies, emeralds, and sapphires, which can be
seen along the hem of St Barbara's cloak. These
ornamentations were fixed not with lead but with a
thick layer of paint which was applied prior to firing.
Consequently, many of these inclusions have
subsequently been lost, with only vacant spaces
hinting towards this panel's former splendour.

Adam and Eve, about 1500
Probably made in the southern Netherlands,
now Belgium
Colourless glass, vitreous paint, silver stain,
lead
24.4 cm x 24.4 cm x 1 cm
45.445

With the introduction of the printing press into
Europe in the fifteenth century, stained glass
designers could borrow and adapt imagery from
a growing range of commercially produced books
and prints.

This roundel, showing the Temptation of Adam and
Eve and their subsequent Expulsion from Eden, is
copied directly from a woodcut by Michel Wolgemut
(1434–1519), produced for the *Liber Chronicarum*,
commonly known as the *Nuremberg Chronicle*
(published 1493).

The prominent breaks in this piece date to the time
of the roundel's painting, as is apparent by the
discovery of paint within the cracks. That such
imperfections did not result in disposal is proof of
the value of stained glass, both then and now.

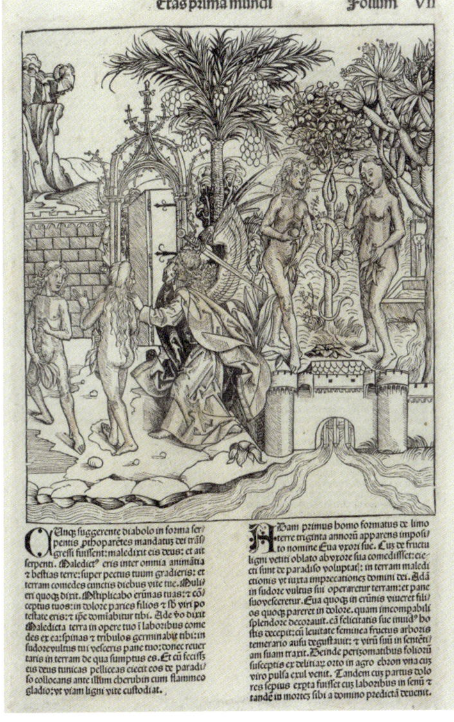

4.5, Detail from the *Nuremberg Chronicle*, 1493,
by Anton Koberger
© CSG CIC Glasgow Museums and Libraries Collections

Objects in Focus

Scenes from the Life of St John the Baptist, about 1510
Probably made in Rouen, France
Colourless glass, pot metal glass, vitreous paint, silver stain, lead
202 cm x 405 cm x 1 cm
Possibly from the Church of St Jean, Rouen, Normandy, France
Showing Zechariah's Vision in the Temple, The Visitation, The Birth of St John the Baptist, St John Taking Leave of his Parents, St John Baptizing Believers, The Rebuking of Herod, Salomé Dancing before Herod, Salomé with the Head of St John
45.417-424

Possibly from the now lost church of St Jean, Rouen (see also p.58), these lights present eight events from the Life of St John the Baptist. Beginning with his father Zechariah's vision foretelling of his birth, the cycle ends with the martyred Baptist's head presented on a platter before the triumphant Herodias.

This window, as with many other surviving examples of continental European glass now in private and public collections, was imported into England by the German-born, Norwich-based weaver and cloth merchant John Christopher Hampp (1750–1825).

Taking advantage of temporary lulls in European warfare, Hampp travelled to the continent in the early nineteenth century, buying substantial amounts of glass from numerous churches, monasteries, and cathedrals – many secularized, closed, or demolished in the wake of the French Revolution and Napoleonic invasion. In Britain, Hampp's extraordinary assemblage of glass appealed to a growing market

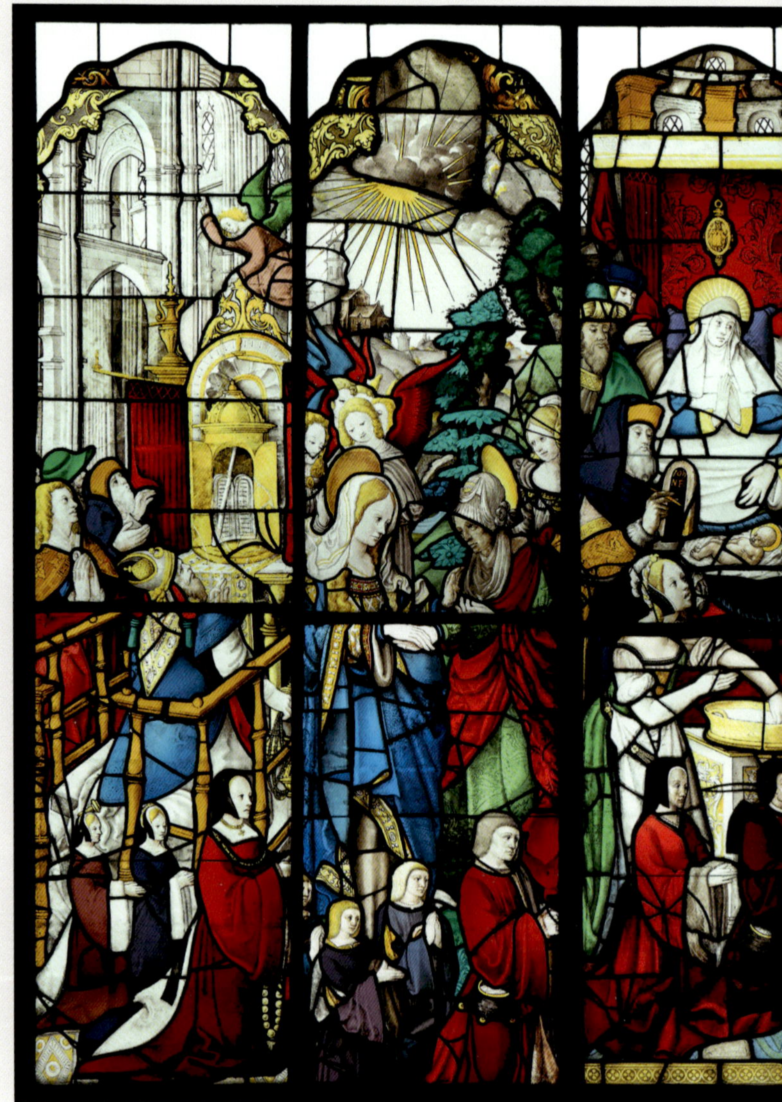

of wealthy and enthusiastic collectors who embraced the aesthetics of the flourishing Gothic revivalist style.

Prior to Burrell's acquisition of these panels in 1946, they had been erected in the long gallery of Blithfield Hall, Staffordshire. Not long after their purchase, Burrell briefly considered donating them to Glasgow Cathedral but had abandoned the idea by September 1947.

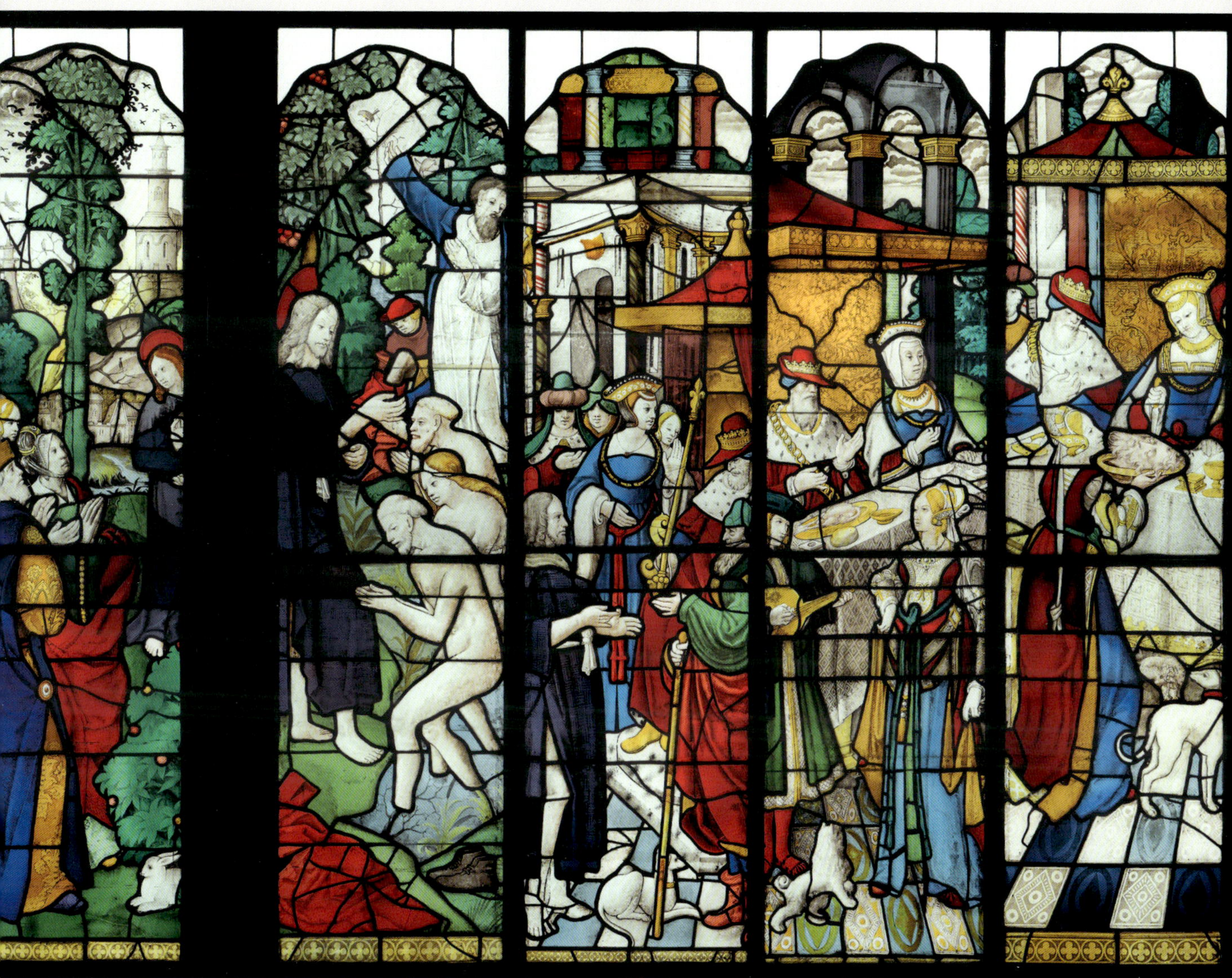

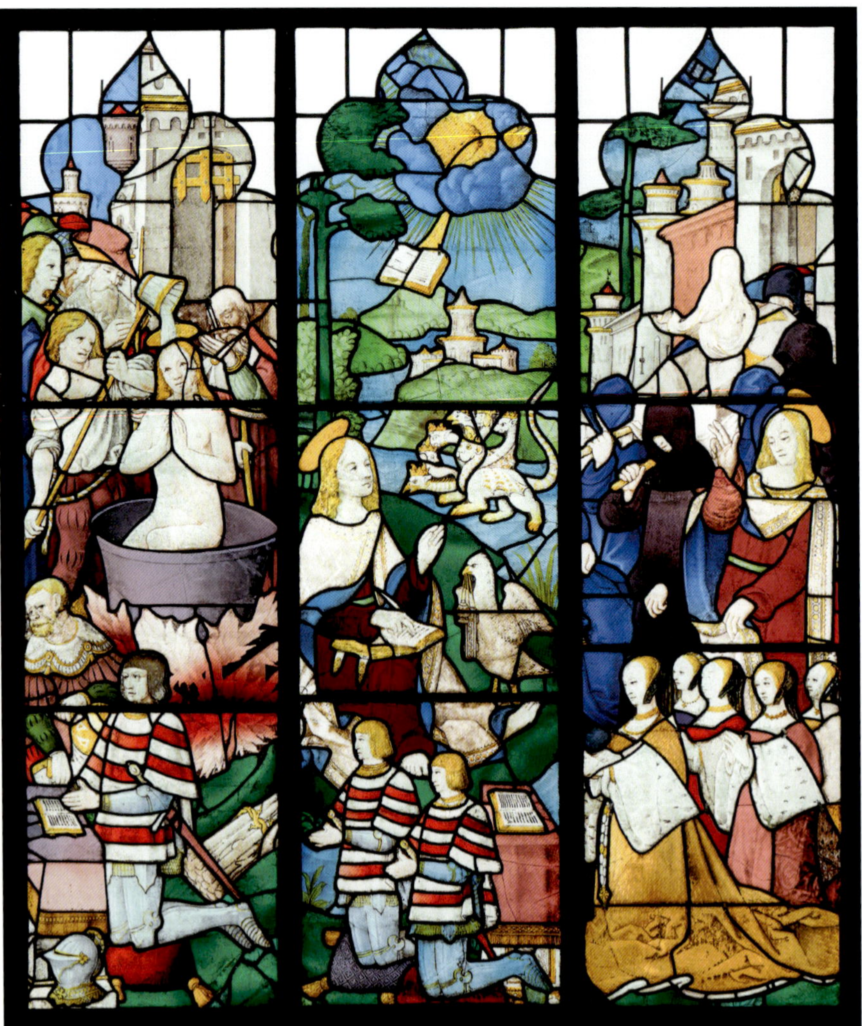

Scenes from the Life of St John the Evangelist, about 1510

Probably made in Rouen, France,
possibly from the workshop of Arnoult de Nimègue
Colourless glass, pot metal glass, vitreous paint,
silver stain, lead
Overall: 226 cm x 64.5cm x 1 cm
Possibly from the Church of St Jean, Rouen, France
Showing St John the Evangelist in a Vat of Boiling
Oil, Writing the Book of Revelation while in exile on
Patmos, and reviving Drusiana
45.390–392

The convincing use of perspective and the
accomplished pictorial style of these panels illustrating
events from the life of St John the Evangelist has seen
them linked to the influential workshop of Netherlandish-
stained glass artist Arnoult de Nimègue (fl. about
1490–about 1536). Nimègue took up residency in
Rouen in 1502 and was responsible for several high-
profile glazing programmes in the city. Other panels
from this cycle can be found at Wells Cathedral,
Somerset, and Ely Cathedral, Cambridgeshire.

The donors of this window, seen along the bottom
of the Glasgow panels, have been identified via their
striped heraldic tabards as members of the Bigars de
la Londe family of Rouen.

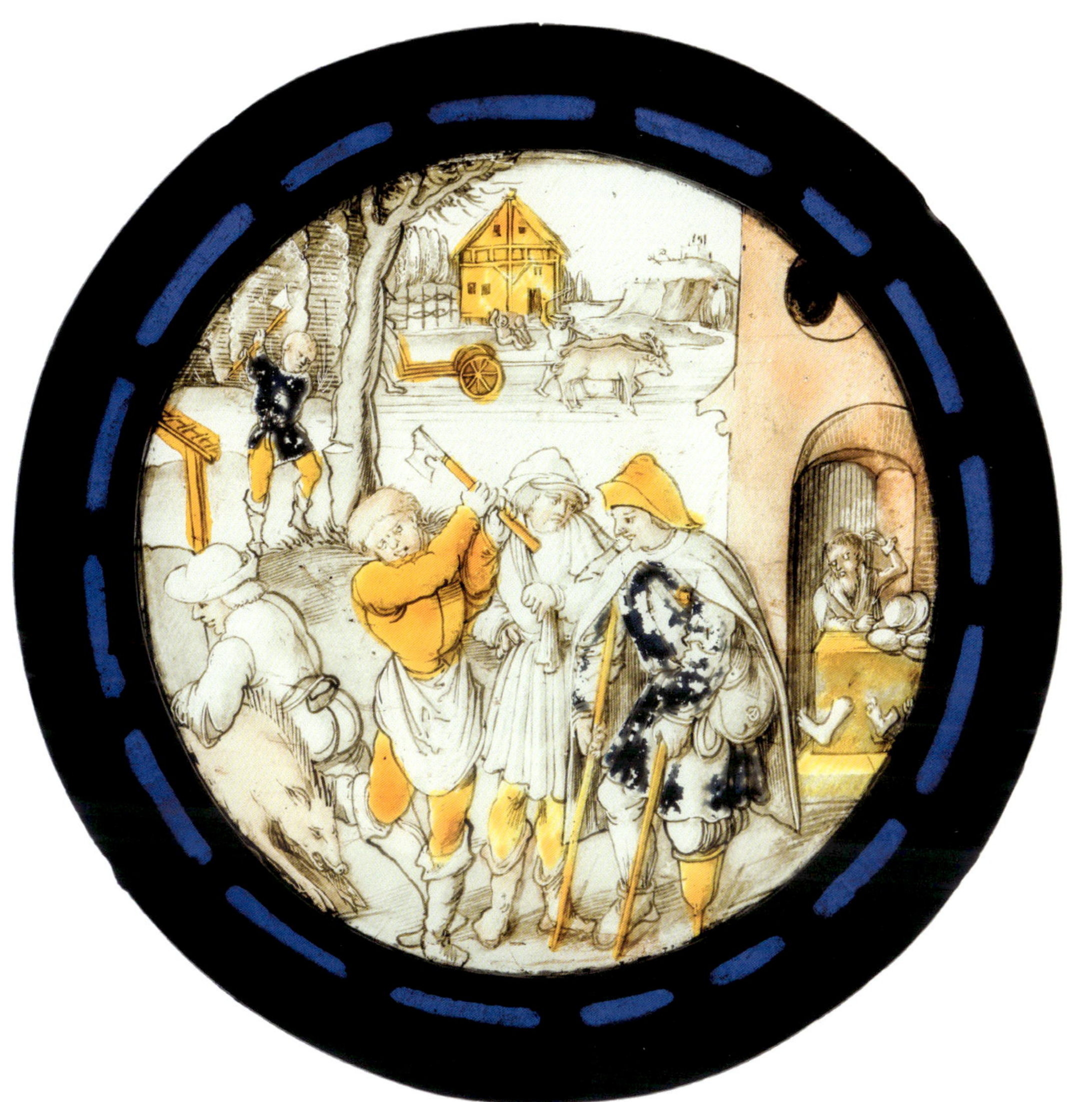

Saturn's Children, 1512–16
Made in Augsburg, southern Germany, now Bavaria, Germany
Design by Jorg Breu the Elder (about 1475–1537)
Colourless glass, pot metal glass (surround), vitreous paint, silver stain, lead
21.2 cm x 21.2 cm x 1 cm
45.494

In the Middle Ages it was thought that the planets and their positions in the heavens influenced human nature and earthly affairs. This small and complex roundel is understood to derive from a larger 'Children of the Planets' series. It represents the personalities, physical characteristics, and activities associated with those born under the influence of Saturn, the furthest, coldest, and slowest moving of the known planets.

Children born under Saturn were, according to commonly held beliefs, inclined to a life of melancholy and misfortune. As seen in this roundel, they had an affinity towards agricultural labour, criminal activities, and were often portrayed as impoverished and susceptible to ill health.

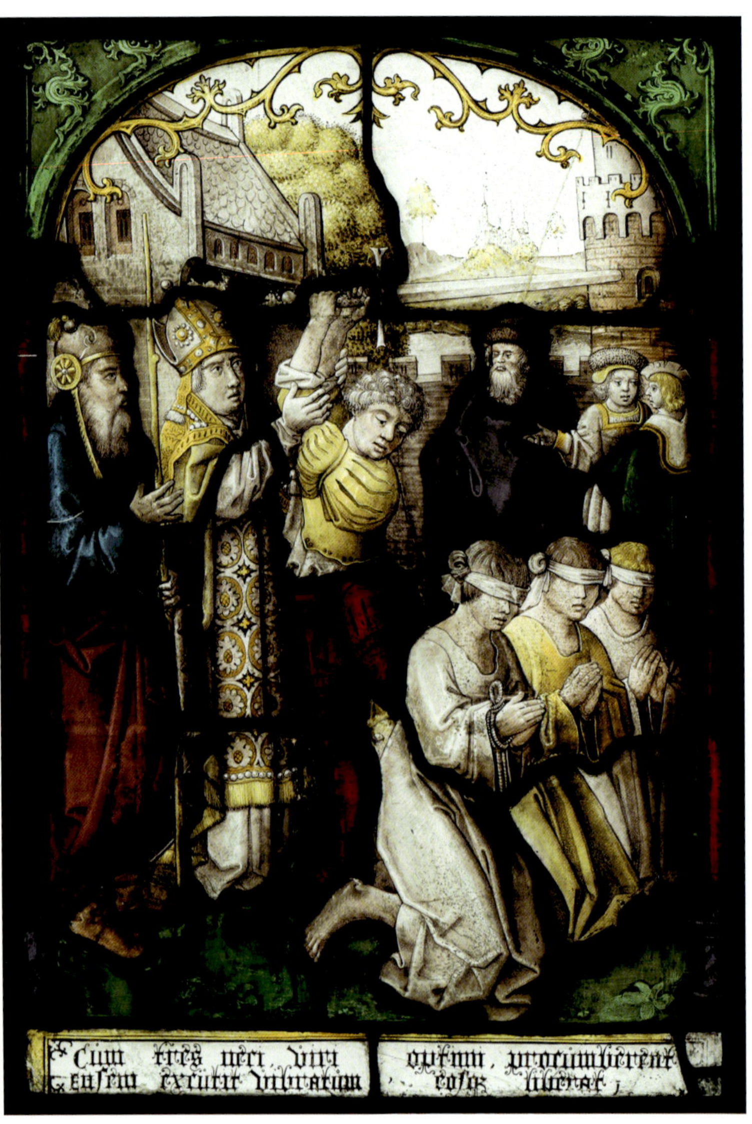

St Nicholas Saving Three Men,
about 1520–25
Made in Brabant, southern Netherlands,
now Belgium
Colourless glass, pot metal glass,
vitreous paint, silver stain, lead
69.5 cm x 48.7 cm x 1 cm
From the Charterhouse of Louvain,
Brabant, southern Netherlands
45.471

Dressed in lavish clerical vestments,
St Nicholas, the fourth-century Bishop
of Myra, stays the arm of an executioner
who readies himself to behead three
falsely accused captives.

This is one of six surviving panels from
the Great Cloister of the Charterhouse
of Louvain. It is from a series financed
by Nicolaas Ruterius, Bishop of Arras
(1442–1509), dedicated to the life and
miracles of his patron saint.

Along with others from this commission,
this panel can be traced back to the
collection of Sir Thomas Neave (1761–
1848), Baronet of Dagnam Park, Essex,
an early collector and connoisseur of
medieval and Renaissance stained glass.

The Meeting of Saints Joachim and Anne at the Golden Gate, about 1520

Made in France
Colourless glass, pot metal glass, vitreous paint, silver stain, lead
159 cm x 67.8 cm x 1 cm
Made in France
45.389.a-b

The parents of the Virgin Mary, the elderly St Joachim and St Anne, embrace beneath the Golden Gate of Jerusalem. Traditionally, this meeting marks the moment of the Virgin Mary's own immaculate, and divinely ordained, miraculous conception.

Details of Mary's parentage and early life are not mentioned in the New Testament but derive from sources such as the the *Proto-evangelium of James* (about 150 AD) and the *Gospel of Pseudo-Matthew* (about 600–650 AD), religious texts that supplemented the limited biographical information offered by a reading of the Bible. Elaborating on the Gospel narrative, these texts offered insight into Mary's infancy and childhood and provided greater detail and inspiration for the medieval artist.

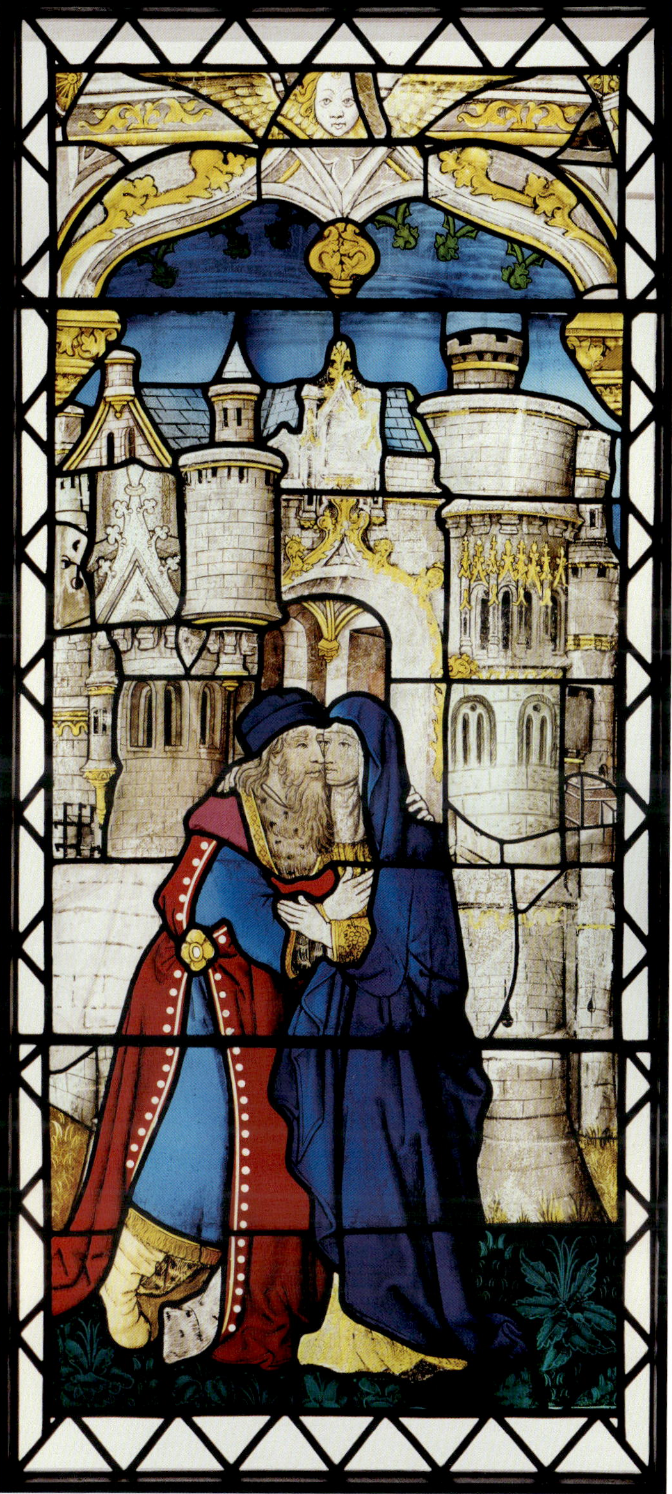

Tree of Jesse, about 1520
Made in Rouen, France
Colourless glass, pot metal glass, vitreous paint,
silver stain, lead
Clear, coloured, stained and painted glass, lead
Overall (both): 190.5 cm x 69 cm x 1 cm
45.393–394

'Tree of Jesse' windows portray the genealogy of
Christ, and his descent from the Old Testament
patriarch Jesse, as it was prophesied in the biblical
Book of Isaiah (11:1). They have been popular since
the very earliest Gothic glazing schemes of the
twelfth century. The tree's twisting stylized branches
are inhabited by Christ's ancestors, including the
biblical king, David, son of Jesse, who is identified
by his golden harp.

These windows were probably once part of a three-
light arrangement; a now missing central panel is
likely to have depicted the tree springing from the
figure of Jesse and culminating in Christ and the
Virgin Mary.

The original location of these panels is yet to be
established but by the early nineteenth century they
were installed in the chapel at Costessey Hall, Norfolk.
The chapel at Costessey was built in 1809 by Sir
William Jerningham (1736–1809). It was home to a
large and important collection of historical stained
glass, from which Burrell was to acquire some 18
windows. Described by the stained glass restorer
and cataloguer of the Costessey Collection, Maurice
Drake (1875–1923), as the 'showpiece' of the
Costessey glass, this window was acquired by
Sir William around 1920. Installed in the drawing
room at Hutton Castle in 1928, these panels were
amongst the earliest stained glass to be installed
there, setting an early high standard for Burrell's
domestic glazing scheme.

Interior of Hutton Castle, Drawing Room. Photography by
Rupert Roddam, 1949.
© Glasgow Museums Archive, GMA.2013.1.1.1116

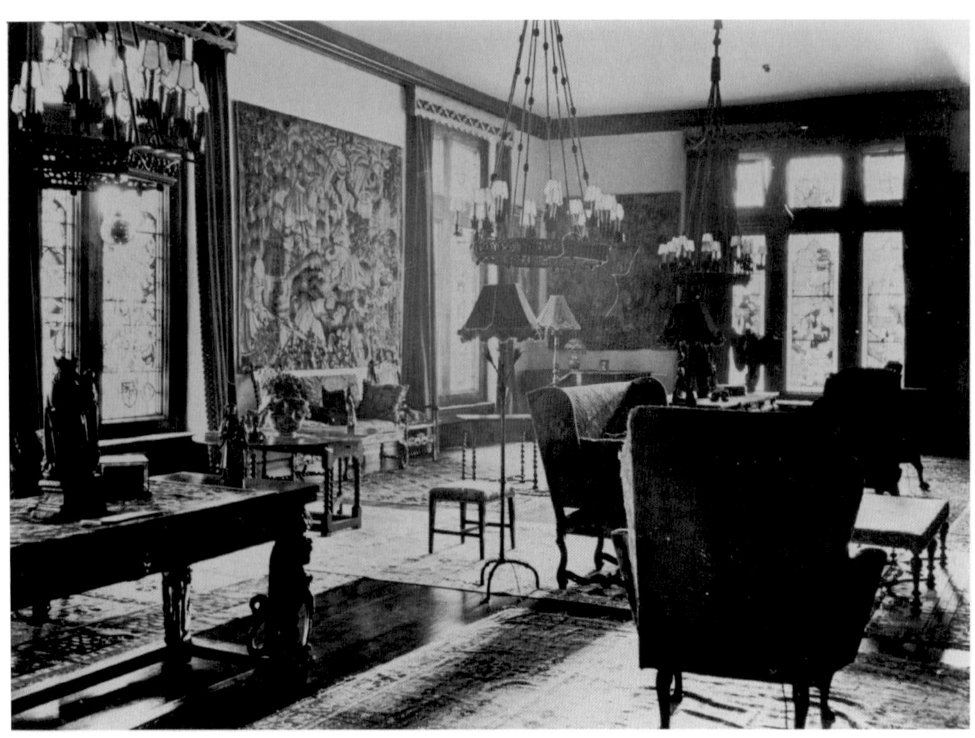

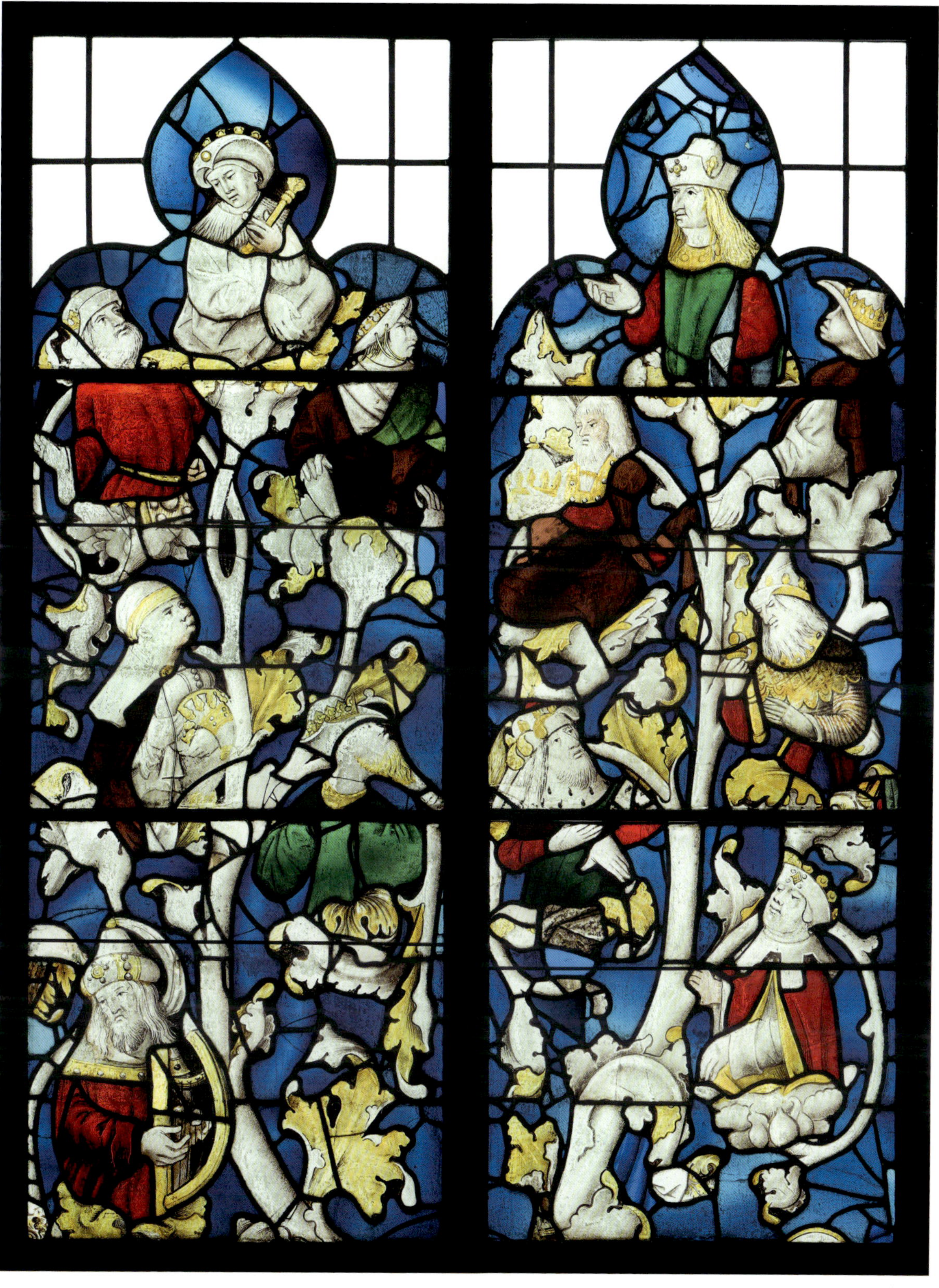

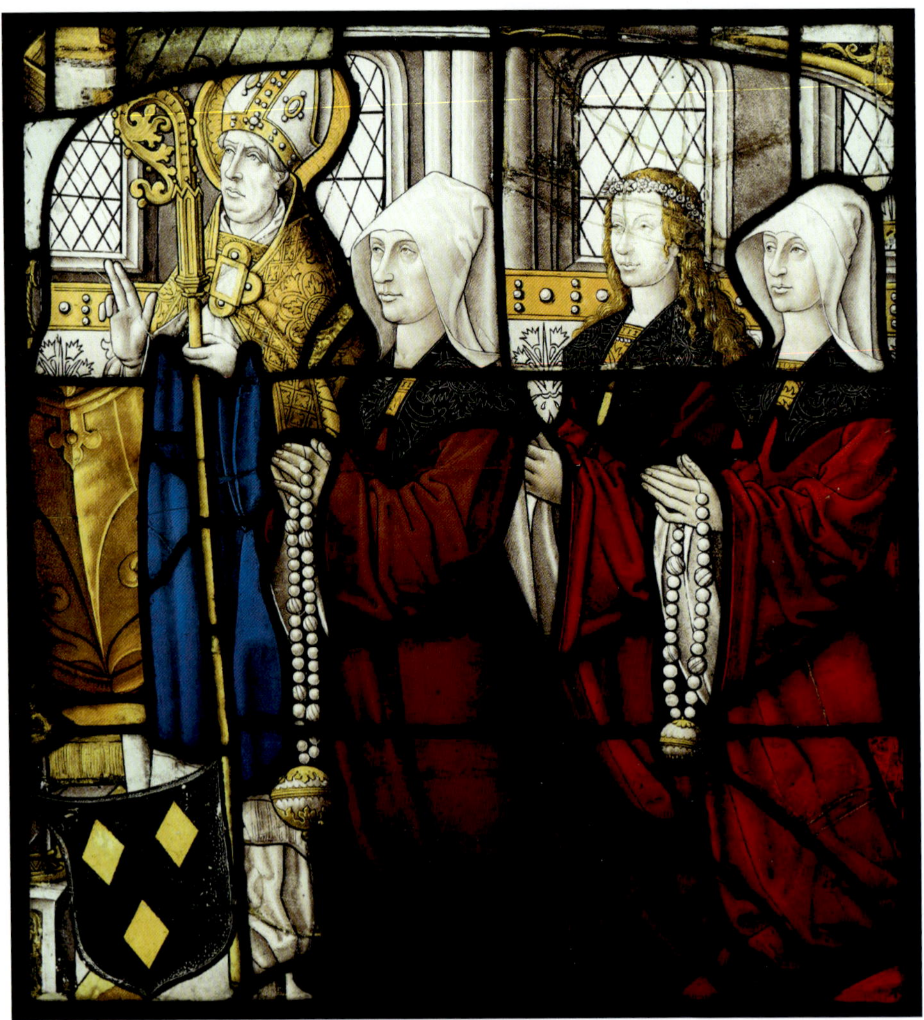

Three Female Donors and Patron Saint,

about 1524–26
Made in Cologne, Germany
Colourless glass, pot metal glass, vitreous paint,
silver stain, lead
64.3 cm x 59.7 cm x 1 cm
From the Cistercian cloister of St Apern, Cologne,
Germany
45.436

Unlike earlier donor panels with their somewhat generic approach towards donors' features (see p.8), this remarkable piece is delicately painted with nuanced, captivating, life-like detail. Alongside an unidentified bishop saint, three female donors, a mother and her daughters, kneel in a church before a late Gothic, lattice-glazed window. Two of the figures, their heads covered, hold rosaries. The third wears a chaplet of flowers above loose flowing hair, denoting that she is unmarried. The fleshy and rounded facial features suggest that the painter of this panel was influenced by the contemporary work of Cologne's foremost portrait painter, Barthel Bruyn the Elder (1493–1555).

The Annunciation, about 1525

Made in the southern Netherlands, now Belgium
Colourless glass, vitreous paint, silver stain, lead
23.4 cm x 23.4 cm x 1 cm
45.442

Small-scale roundels, such as this Annunciation
scene, were manufactured on a near industrial scale
from the late fifteenth to mid-sixteenth century, with
notable centres of production in the Low Countries
– an area largely corresponding with modern-day
Belgium and the Netherlands.

Such roundels were made predominately for private
and secular spaces, often within the homes of
northern Europe's burgeoning mercantile classes.
They were intended to be viewed at close range and
could be painted with meticulous detail that rivalled
contemporary drawings and panel paintings. In this
sophisticated example, yellow silver stain, layered
paint washes, and brush applied stipple-shading
produce subtle depth and shadow.

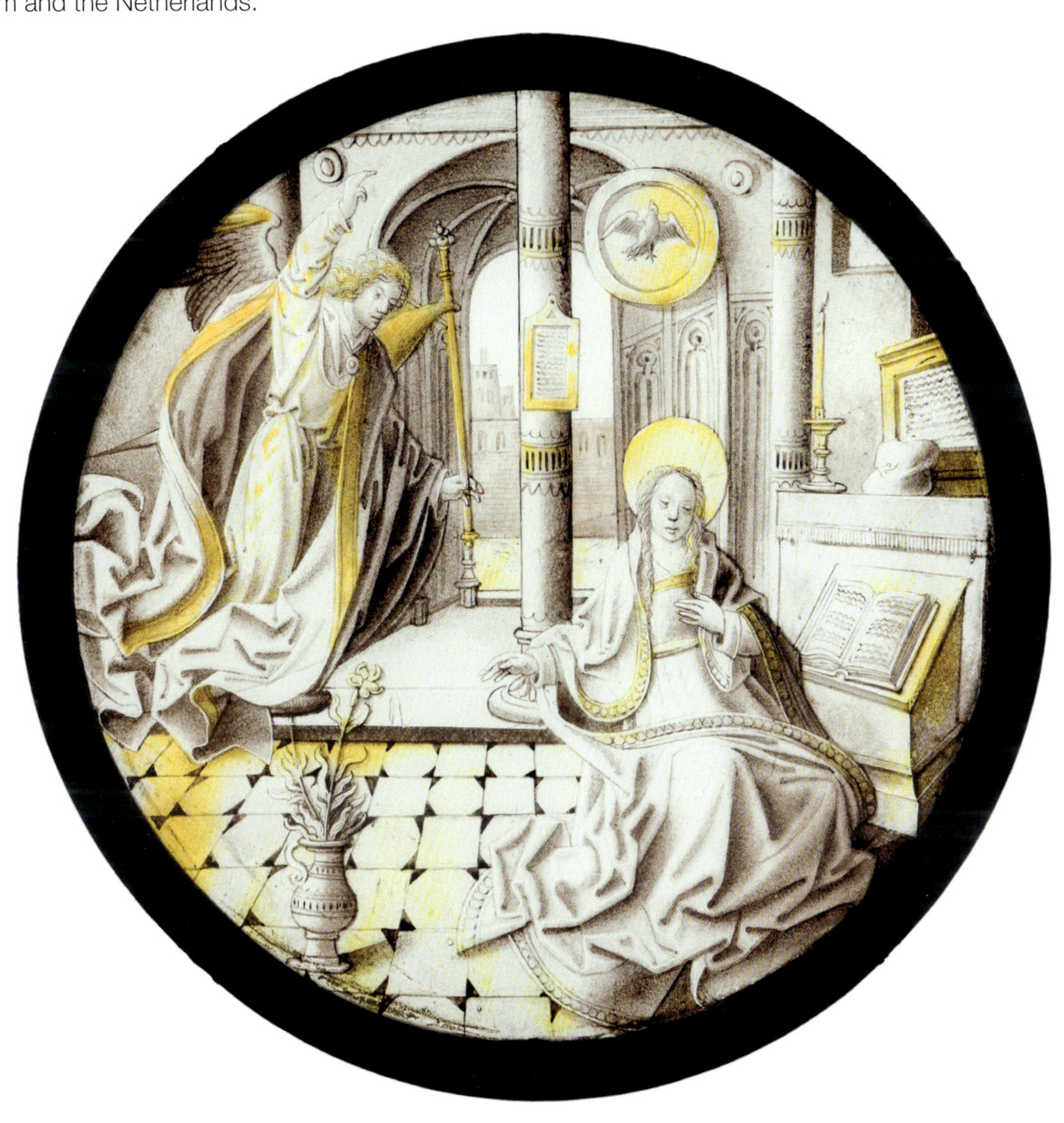

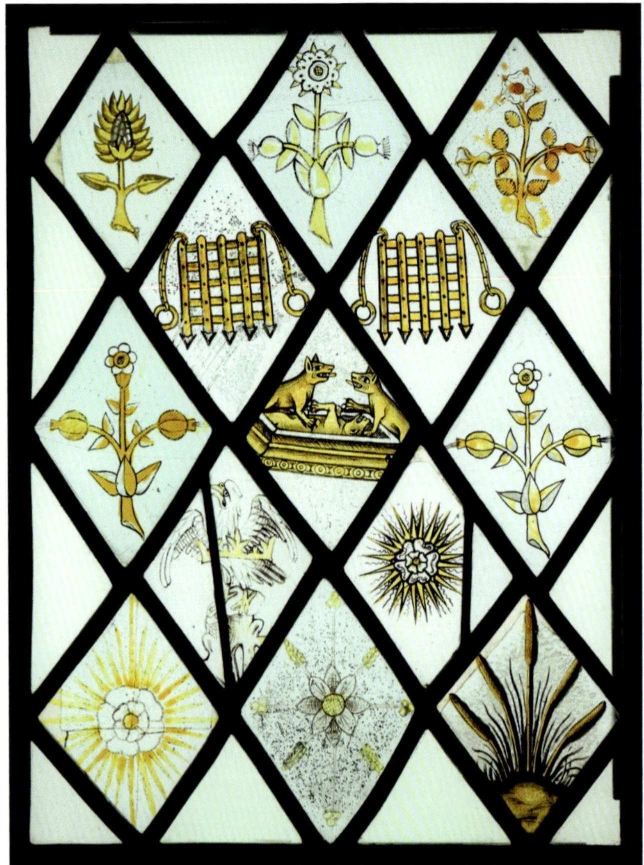

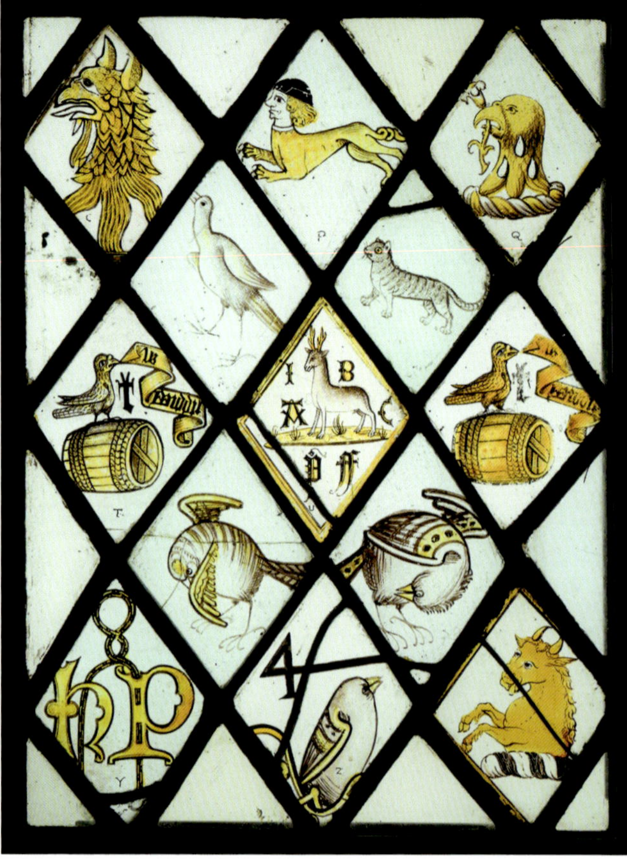

Quarries, 1400–1600

Made in England
Colourless glass, vitreous paint, silver stain, lead
45.3 cm x 34 cm x 1 cm
53.5 cm x 42 cm x 1 cm
45.102.a, 45.102.b

Possibly deriving from the French word '*carré*', meaning 'square', quarries are small square or diamond-shaped panels incorporated into the latticework of larger windows. They were often employed as a decorative surrounding to more colourful, frequently armorial, pieces. Made from clear glass and simply modelled with black-brown paints and yellow silver stain, they offered a cheaper alternative to more complex, multi-coloured glass, and were encountered in both secular and ecclesiastical settings.

These windows are composites of fifteenth- and sixteenth-century examples, emblazoned with a variety of motifs, including crests, royal badges, and rebuses – heraldic devices that carry visual puns derived from family names.

Rebus of John Islip, Abbot of Westminster,

about 1500–32
Made in England
Colourless glass, vitreous paint, silver stain, lead
31 cm x 24.5 cm x 1 cm
Westminster Abbey, London, England
45.223

This diamond-shaped quarry depicts a visual pun or
rebus on the name of John Islip (b.1464), Abbot of
Westminster from 1500 until his death in 1532.
In addition to the references to his name presented
by the eye and word 'SLIP', the pun is further
reinforced by the figure of a man slipping down
the central tree's trunk. Thin branch cuttings,
known as 'slips', are also seen in his hands,
and lying upon the ground at the base
of the tree.

This panel may have originated
from Westminster Abbey,
where a chantry chapel
built by Abbot Islip is
decorated with other
iterations of his rebus.

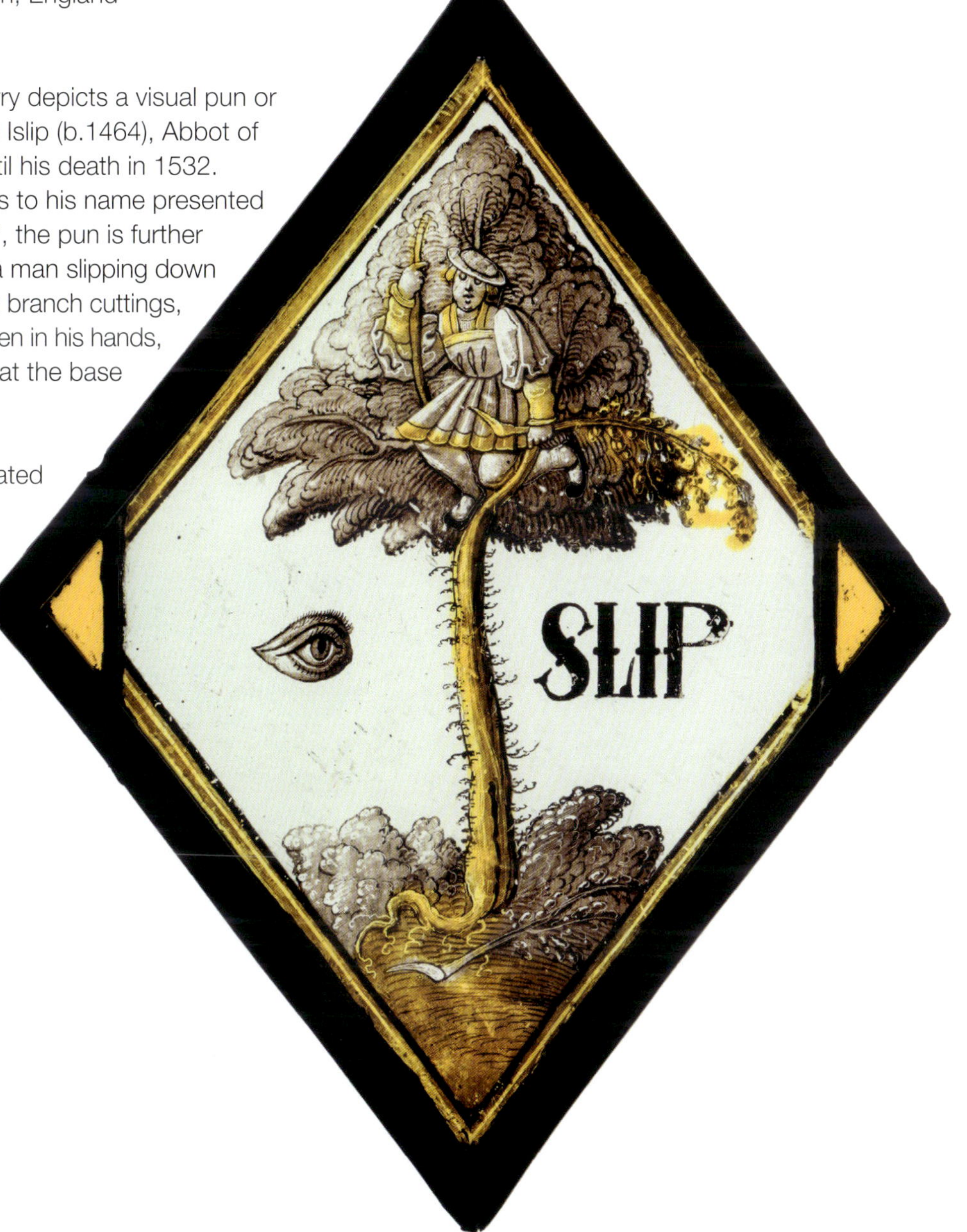

Triple Rose, about 1530
Made in England
Colourless glass, pot metal glass, vitreous paint, lead
27.3 cm x 27.3 cm x 1 cm
45.97

Emblematic of the union between the Lancastrian king Henry Tudor (1457–1509) and his wife, Elizabeth of York (1466–1503), the conjoining of the heraldic red and white roses of the royal houses of Lancaster and York was a potent and enduring symbol of the House of Tudor.

Presented here as a triple rose, this unusual configuration is an extraordinary exemplar of the glazier's precision and expertise. Approached with great dexterity and delicacy, in a process known as 'insertion', the glass has been adeptly cut through, allowing for the intricate placement and leading of the various distinct layers of the rose.

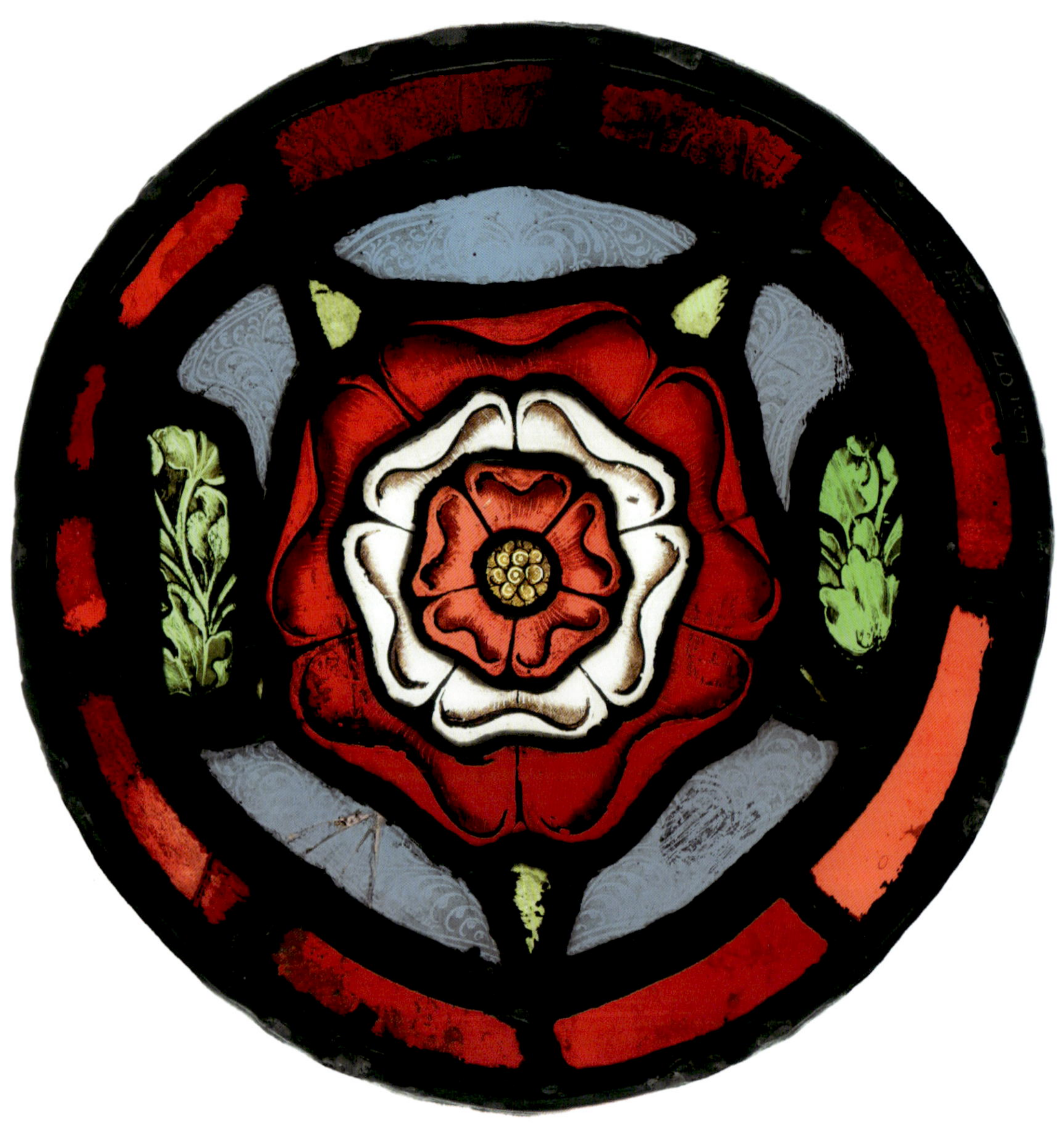

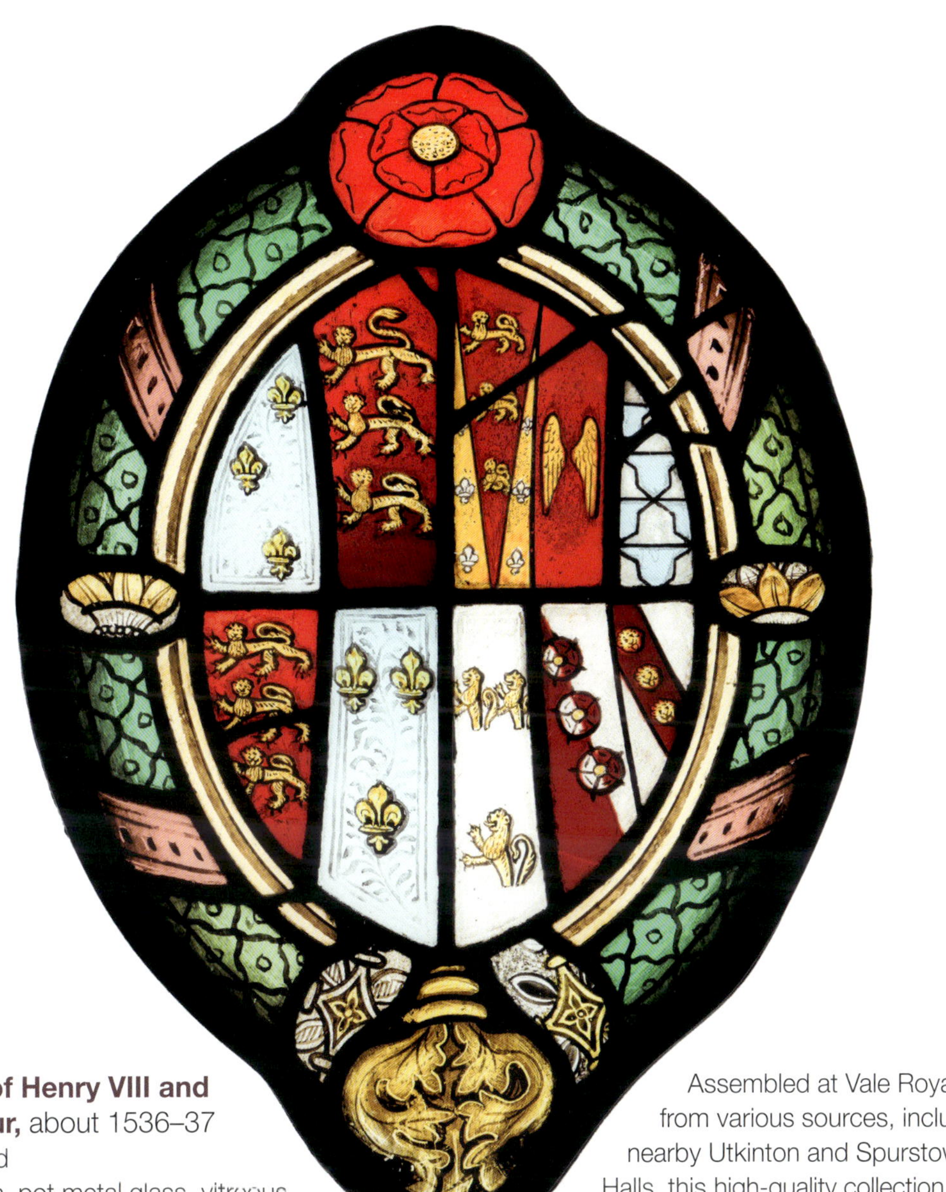

Royal Arms of Henry VIII and Jane Seymour, about 1536–37

Made in England
Colourless glass, pot metal glass, vitreous paint, silver stain, lead
42.5 cm x 30.6 cm
From Vale Royal Abbey, England
45.255

Purchased for a mere £55 in 1947, Burrell's acquisition of 37, predominantly sixteenth-century armorial roundels and panels from Vale Royal Abbey, Cheshire, ranks amongst his greatest bargains.

Assembled at Vale Royal from various sources, including nearby Utkinton and Spurstow Halls, this high-quality collection includes royal shields and heraldic arms of Cheshire's gentry.

Royal arms, such as this example representing the arms of King Henry VIII (1491–1547) quartered (joined) with those of his third wife, Jane Seymour (about 1508–37), were a common feature of sixteenth-century English domestic glazing. Commissioned by the aristocracy and landed gentry, such pieces served as conspicuous declarations of loyalty and allegiance to the Crown.

Objects in Focus

Heraldic panels, 1500–1600
Made in England
From Fawsley Hall, England

One of Burrell's last acquisitions of stained glass, these panels come from a series of 39 heraldic shields from Fawsley Hall, Northamptonshire. Burrell, having first been alerted to the panels in 1938, patiently pursued this glass for over a decade, finally securing them for the collection in 1950.

Commissioned in the sixteenth century by successive generations of the Knightley family of Fawsley, these superb panels once formed part of an extensive armorial series proclaiming the family's supposed genealogy, prestigious family connections, and alliances.

Several of these panels were inserted into the grand oriel window of Fawsley's Great Hall. At the apex of the window was the largest panel in the series; the elaborate and magnificently preserved shield combining the arms of Sir Edmund Knightley (1491–1542), with those of his wife Ursula de Vere (d.1558), sister and co-heir of John de Vere, 14th Earl of Oxford (1499–1526). These panels represent some of the finest English armorial glass of the age, the highly decorative finish and complex quartering of arms relying on the glazier's ingenuity and mastery of a range of techniques and skills.

The nearby parish church of St Mary the Virgin, Fawsley, is home to several associated heraldic panels presumed to have come from the Hall.

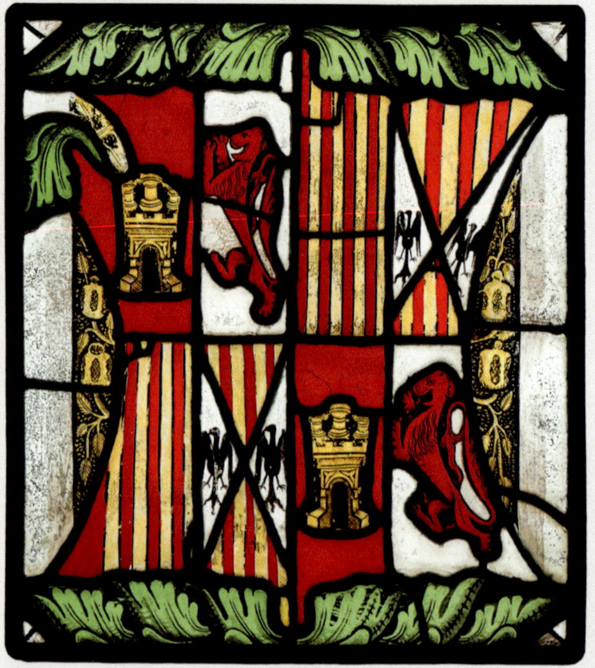

Above: Arms of Catherine of Aragon, first wife of King Henry VIII of England, and Queen of England from 1509–33, about 1510–30
Colourless glass, pot metal glass, vitreous paint, silver stain, lead
45.7 cm x 40.6 cm x 1 cm
45.308

Right: Arms of John de Vere (1442–1513), 13th Earl of Oxford, P.C., K.G. about 1540
Colourless glass, pot metal glass, vitreous paint, silver stain, lead
41.3 cm x 41.3 cm x 1 cm
45.325

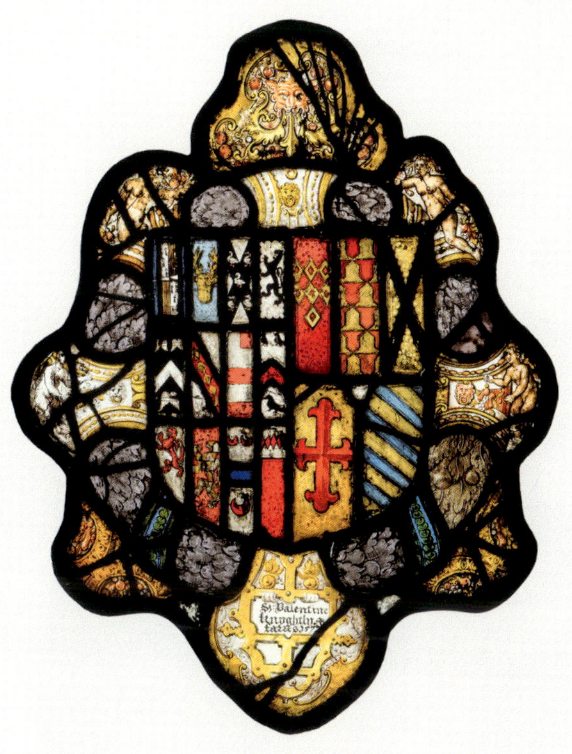

Arms of Sir Valentine Knightley (d.1566) of Fawsley Hall and Anne Ferrers (d.1554), about 1572
Colourless glass, pot metal glass, vitreous paint, silver stain, lead
63 cm x 48.5 cm x 1 cm
45.319

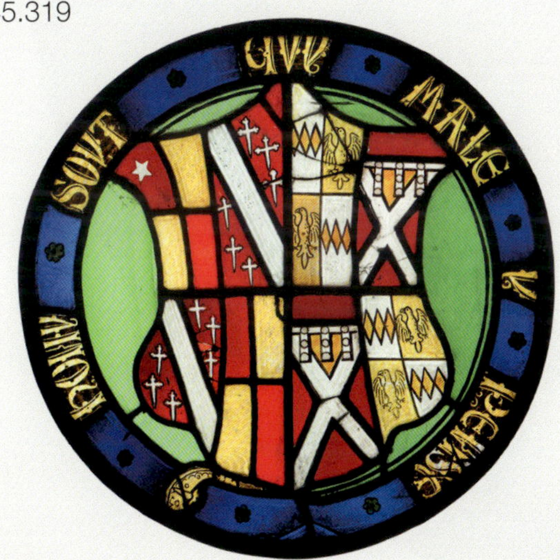

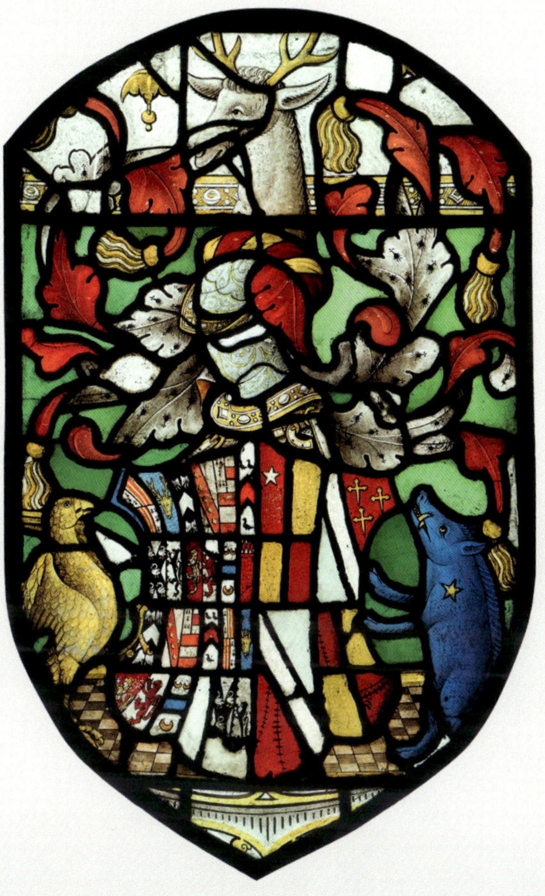

Arms of Knightley impaling de Vere quartering Howard, about 1540
Colourless glass, pot metal glass, vitreous paint, silver stain, lead
80.5 cm x 50.5 cm x 1 cm
45.332

The largest shield in the Fawsley Hall series, these arms represent the marriage of Sir Edmund Knightley and Ursula de Vere. The rendering of complex arms such as these was a demanding and laborious task. The expertly worked flashed red and blue glass has been carefully abraded and silver stained to enable the intricate detail of the blazon.

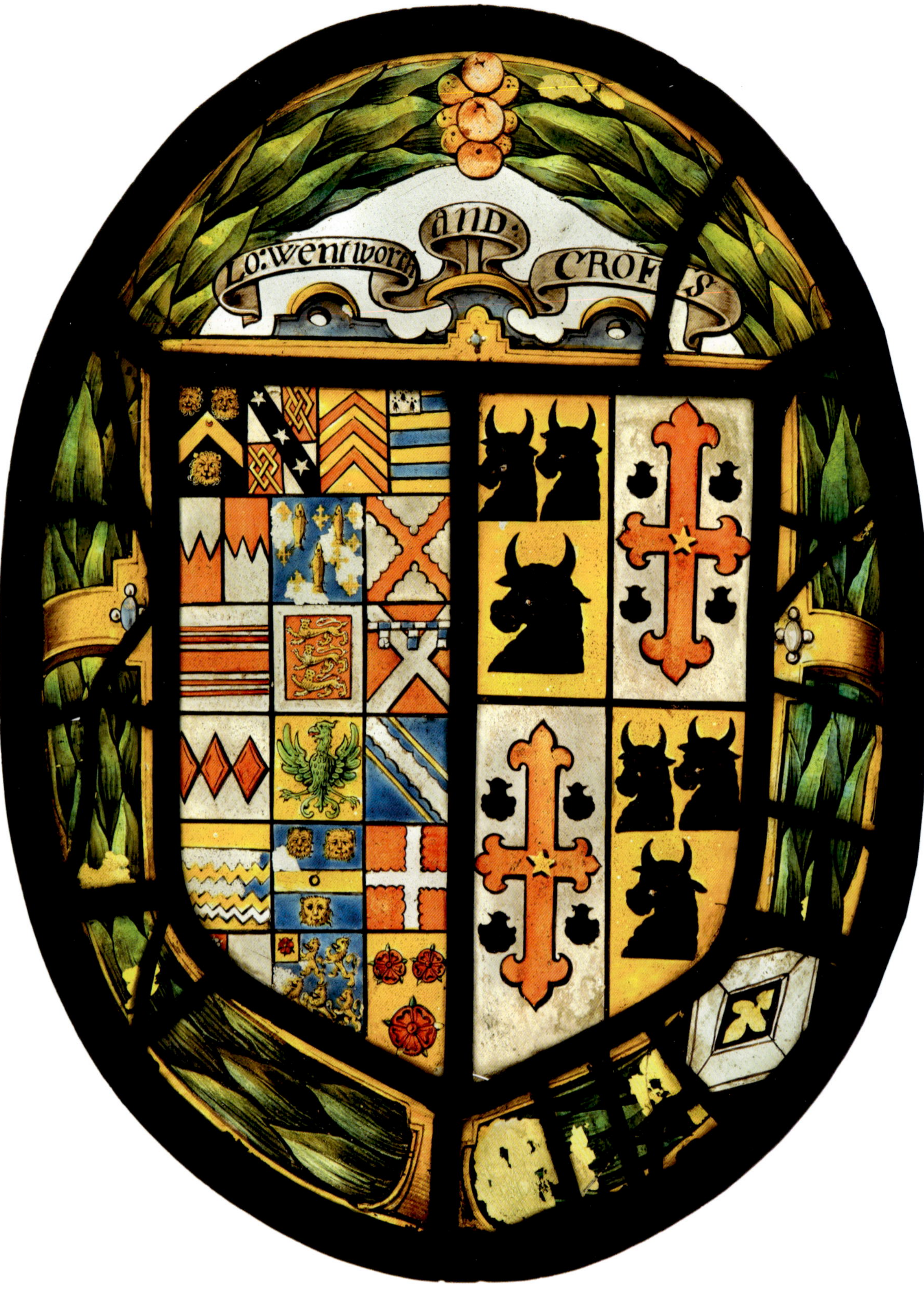

72

Seventeenth-century Glass

Large commissions for churches and religious houses remained scarce in post-Reformation Europe. Even in Catholic countries, where stained glass had been spared from the devastation and proscriptions of the previous century, the demand for monumental figurative and colourful stained glass fell into steep decline in the seventeenth century. Across Europe the brooding dark interiors of the Gothic age were no longer desirable and stained glass formed little part of the emerging architectural styles of the Baroque, where plain, clear glazing was preferred.

The market for small-scale domestic and heraldic glass, however, remained buoyant, supported by both noble and aristocratic households and the growing demands of the affluent middle classes. Such glass was made to be viewed at close quarters, and glass painters responded by turning to enamels to produce intimate works full of incident and captivating detail. Some of the finest and most accomplished enamel-painted glass was made in Switzerland, where it became customary to gift or exchange stained glass between religious foundations, civic organizations, and fellow citizens. By the end of the 1600s, with its reliance on enamels, stained glass had come to resemble oil painting on glass, with many of the traditional practices of pot metal glass manufacture and stained glass design abandoned and

eventually forgotten. It would not be until the great 'Gothic Revival' of the eighteenth and nineteenth centuries that medieval methods and techniques would re-emerge, and traditional stained glass studios be re-established.

Burrell obtained glass from several dealers throughout his life, but none were to prove more influential or important to the collection than Wilfred Drake, of the transatlantic stained glass dealership Thomas and Drake. Working with Burrell on the glazing of Hutton Castle from the 1920s, Drake continued to support Burrell's collecting of stained glass for over two decades, acting not just as a dealer but as a trusted consultant, advisor, and broker. An archive of over 700 letters between the two men reveals both Burrell's respect for, and reliance on, Drake as he looked to not only develop his collection but also cultivate his own understanding of the history and significance of his acquisitions. In a letter of 1947, Burrell reflected on his fruitful relationship with Drake, remarking that 'without you, I could not have had so much good glass as you have enabled me to get'.

Although Drake described Burrell as a 'connoisseur of Gothic glass', Sir William was seemingly reticent to enter the stained glass market after Drake's death in 1948. A reading of Burrell's purchase books from 1949 until his own death in 1958 reveals few stained glass purchases, with the most significant being 39 armorial panels from Fawsley Hall (see pp.70, 71), the result of a deal set in motion by Drake some years earlier.

Opposite: Painted directly onto glass, enamels were ideally suited to the crowded quarterings and decorative surrounds that characterized late sixteenth- and seventeenth-century armorial glass. (Detail of 45.352, see p.76)

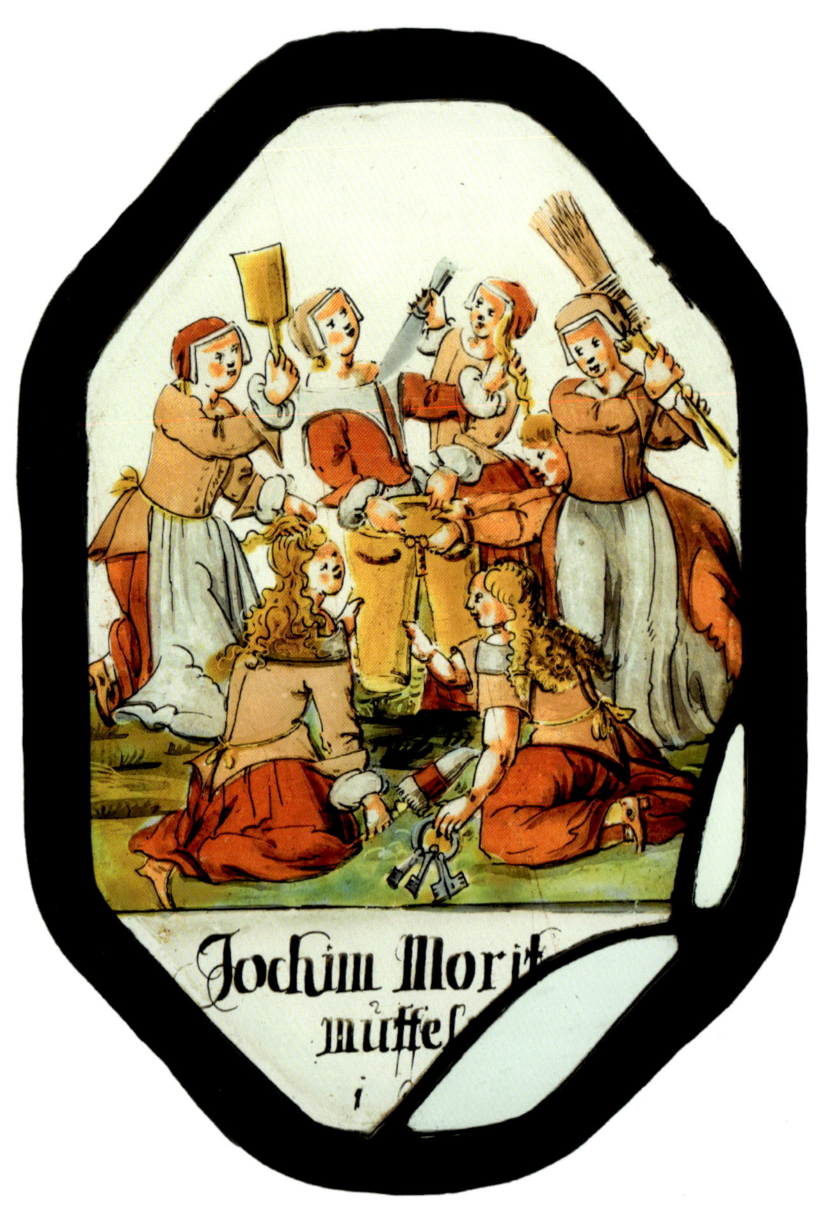

Battle of the Trousers, after 1600
Possibly made in the Dutch Republic,
now the Netherlands, or northern Germany
Colourless glass, enamel paint, silver stain, lead
19.4 cm x 14 cm x 1 cm
45.613

In this farcical panel, seven women engage in a violent brawl over a pair of men's breeches. Variations on the scene, with both men and women fighting over who shall wear the trousers, were produced as mocking satires, lampooning female efforts to usurp male authority and power. Battling not against a man but rather against each other, this alternative scene, a recurring motif of seventeenth-century Dutch art, is understood to be a suggestive commentary on female sexual desire.

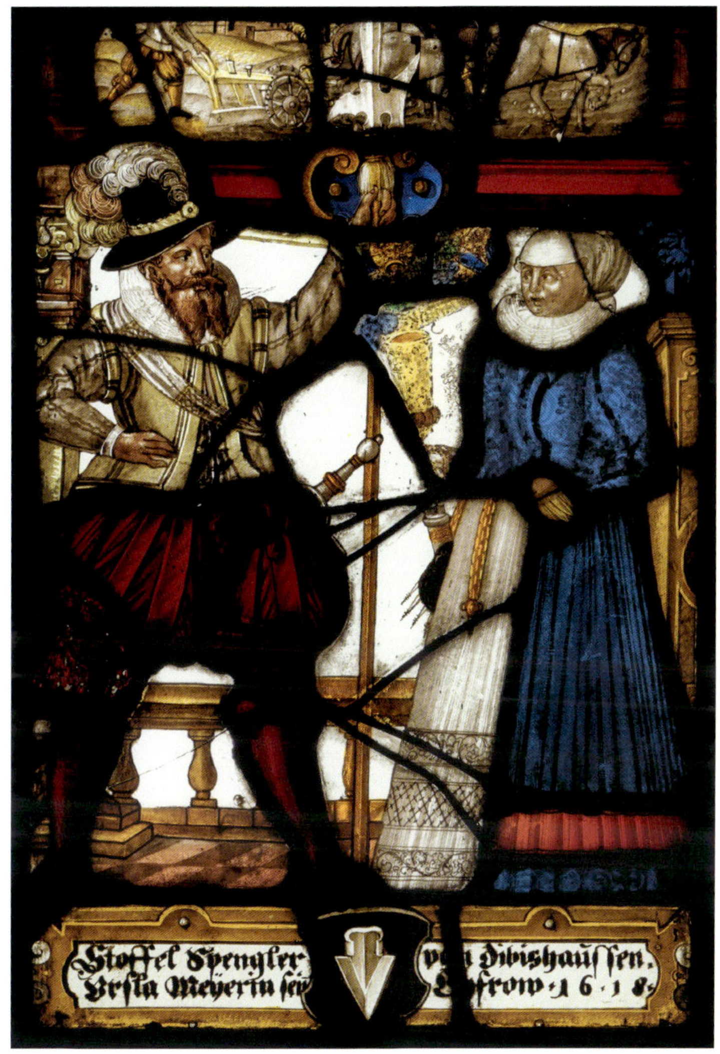

Heraldic glass, depicting Stoffel Spengler of Dibishausen and Ursla Meyerin,

dated 1618
Made in Switzerland
Colourless glass, pot metal, enamel paint, silver stain, lead
30 cm x 21.2 cm x 1 cm
45.528

Known as a '*Willkommscheibe*' or 'Welcome panel', this small-scale piece depicts Stoffel Spengler and his wife Ursla Meyerin, who are identified in the text at the bottom of the panel. Welcome panels were often intended as gifts and were customarily presented upon the completion of a new building or renovation, mounted within a window financed by the donor. Commissioned by a broad clientele to be donated to churches, municipal buildings, and even private houses, 'Welcome panels' were made in great numbers throughout the sixteenth and seventeenth centuries, with the format remaining remarkably consistent.

Armed with a halberd, Spengler is dressed in military attire, symbolic of his role in the civic militia. His wife, in traditional Swiss costume, offers him a chalice, indicative of her role as keeper of the home.

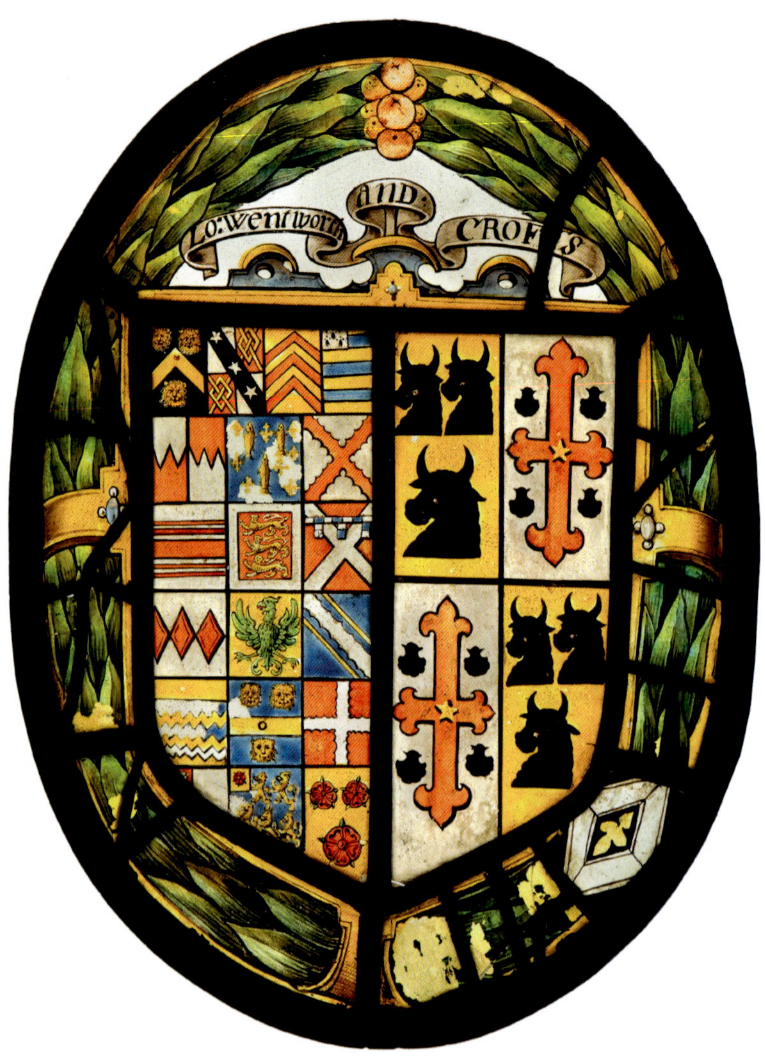

Arms of Wentworth and Crofts,
about 1600–20
Made in Norfolk, England
Colourless glass, enamel paint, silver stain, lead
42 cm x 31.6 cm x 1 cm
From Saxham Hall, Suffolk
45.352

Representing the marriage of Sir Thomas Wentworth, 1st Earl of Cleveland (1591–1667) and his first wife, Anne Crofts (d.1638), this panel is one of a series of seven in the collection understood to have come from Saxham Hall, Suffolk, seat of the Crofts family. An eighth panel, dated to 1620, can be found in the National Gallery of Victoria, Australia.

Likely to have been commissioned by Anne's father, Sir John Crofts (1565–1628), these panels were possibly erected in commemoration or anticipation of a visit by King James VI of Scots and I of England (1566–1625), who was entertained at Saxham Hall on at least three occasions between 1620 and 1622.

Parrot with Plant, 1600–1700
Made in the Dutch Republic, now the Netherlands
Colourless glass, enamel paint, lead
12 cm x 12 cm x 1 cm
45.598

In the seventeenth century, ownership of parrots, and other rare ornamental birds, became synonymous with prosperity, high-status, and sophistication. They were imported into the Dutch Republic via the far-reaching colonialist trade routes of the Dutch East and West India Companies.

This passion for the exotic flora and fauna of newly explored lands was reflected in the arts and in the popularity of ornithological, zoological, and botanical prints and treatises. Many of these prints served as models to other artists, as with this panel, designed after an image of around 1600 ('*Twee papegaaien in een landschap*' – *Two parrots in a landscape*), by the Flemish designer and engraver Adriaen Collaert (about 1560–1618).

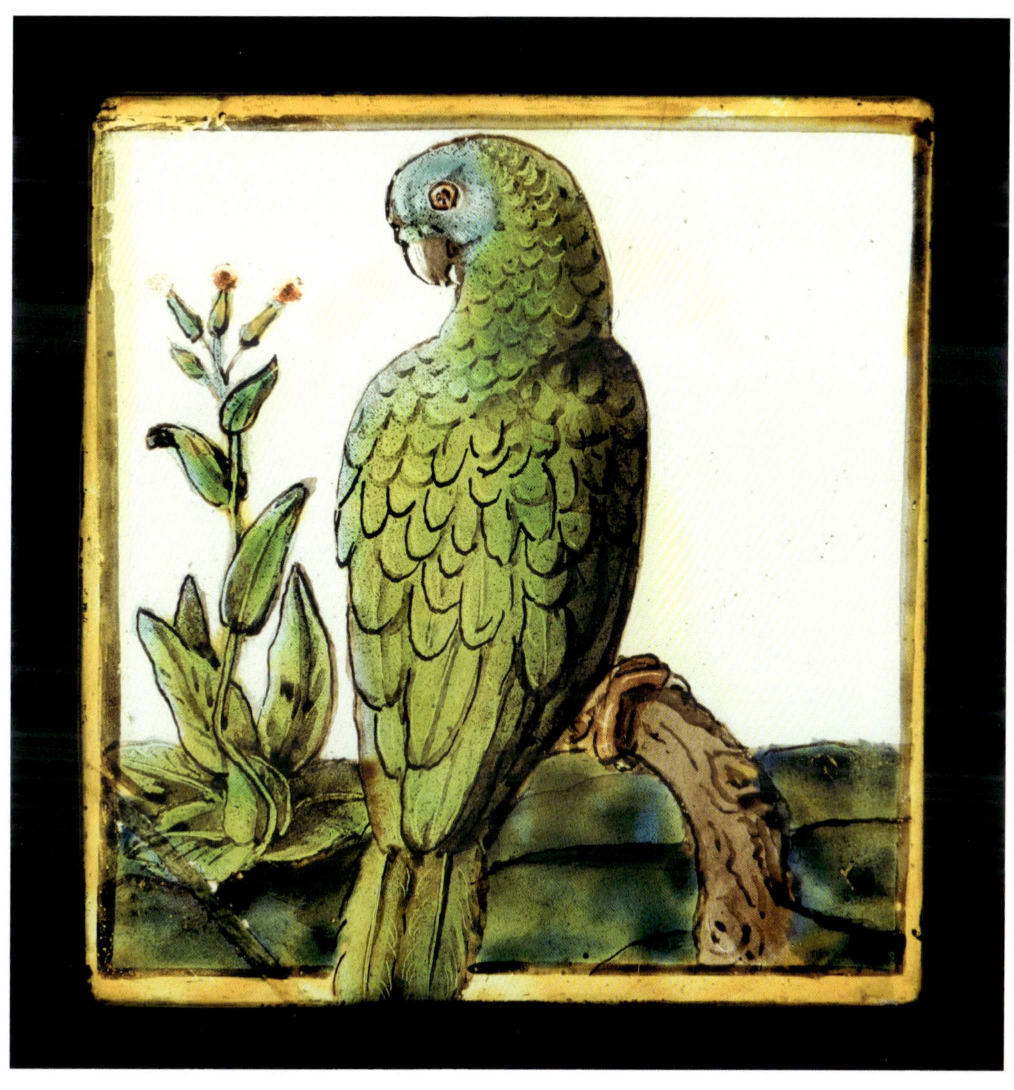

Incidents in the Youth of St Francis,
dated 1671
Made in Zug, Switzerland
From the workshop of Michael Müller IV
Colourless glass, enamel paint, silver stain, lead
19.1 cm x 19.1 cm x 1 cm
45.530

In summer 1941 a quantity of stained glass was removed from Burrell's Glasgow townhouse and transferred to Hutton Castle for wartime safekeeping. Perhaps prompted by the arrival of this glass, Burrell took the opportunity to assess and refine his collection. In July, Sir William sent a box of over 30 examples of Dutch, Swiss, German, and English glass to his stained glass advisor, Wilfred Drake, for appraisal. Burrell remarked that the pieces were 'very unimportant and bought 50 years ago', revealing that they formed some of his earliest stained glass acquisitions.

Drake advised that only four identifiable examples be retained for the collection, including this roundel depicting a scene from the life of St Francis of Assisi. It was painted by one of seventeenth-century Switzerland's most prolific painters of stained glass, Michael Müller IV (d.1682). Evidence from Müller's own records suggests that this roundel once formed part of a 19-part cycle dedicated to the saint. It has been proposed that they were designed for the Franciscan cloister of Maria Opferung, Zug.

Painted with astonishing detail, to the left of the composition St Francis is shown imprisoned within a tower where he is surrounded by monstrous devils and plotting, hellish creatures.

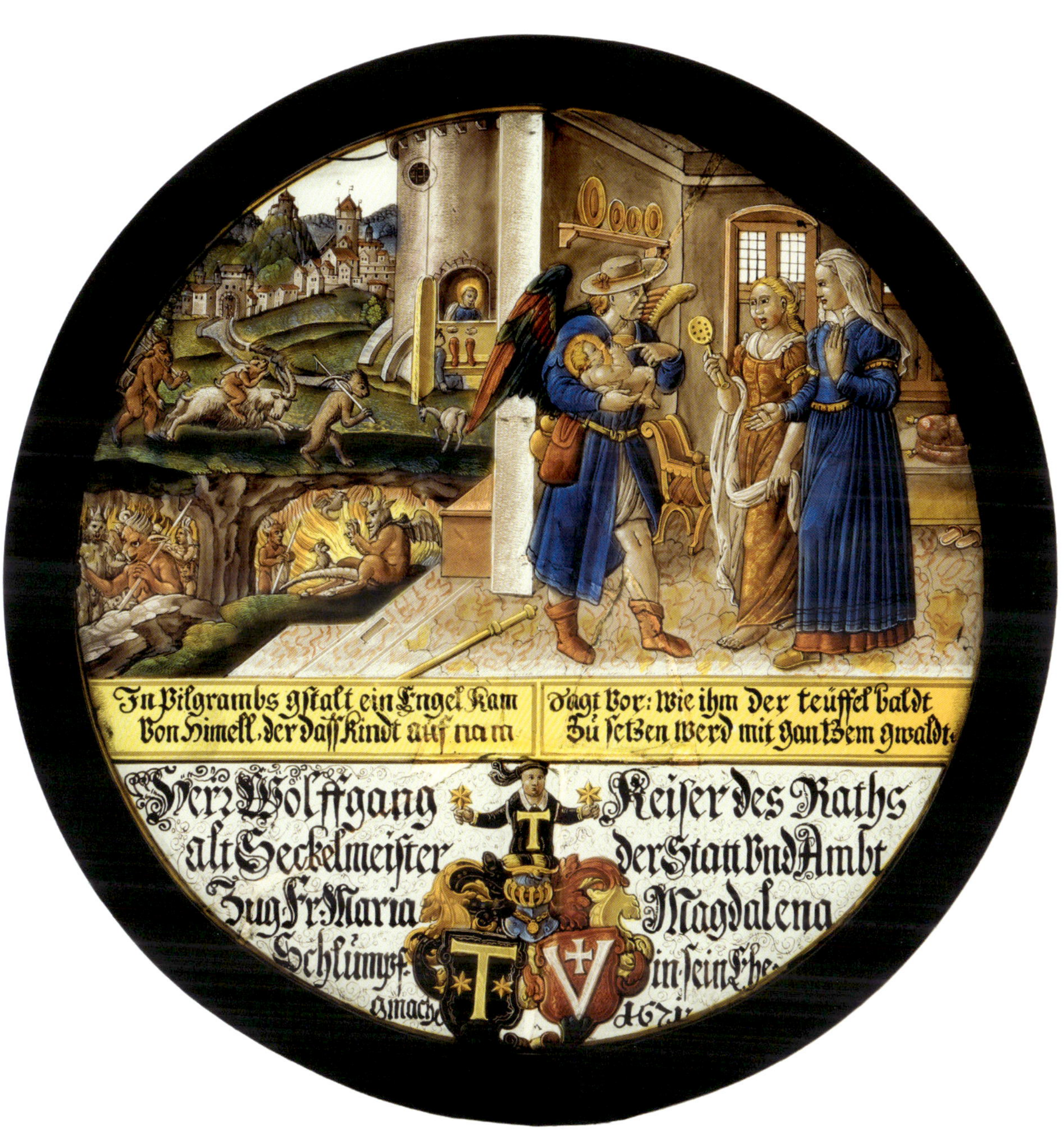
In Pilgrambs gstalt ein Engel kam
von Himell, der dass kindt auff nam
dagt vor: wie ihm der teüffel baldt
zu setzen werd mit gantzem gwaldt
Herr Wolffgang
alt Seckelmeister
zu Fr. Maria
Schlumpf-
gmacht
Keiser des Raths
der Statt vnd Ambt
Magdalena
in sein Ehe-
1671

Further Reading

Martin Bellamy and Isobel MacDonald, *William Burrell: A Collector's Life*, Glasgow Museums and Birlinn, Edinburgh, 2022. Biography of William Burrell, his life, collection and legacy.

Catherine Brisac, *A Thousand Years of Stained Glass*, Macdonald & Co., London, 1986. An extensive and engaging overview of European stained glass. Translated from the original French.

Sarah Brown, *Stained Glass: An Illustrated History*, Bracken Books, London, 1992. A comprehensive introduction to the development of stained glass from its origins to the twentieth century.

Sarah Brown and David O'Connor, *Glass-Painters (Medieval Craftsmen)*, British Museum Press, London, 1991. Insightful and finely illustrated introduction to the working practices of stained glass artists throughout the Middle Ages.

Linda Cannon, *Stained Glass in the Burrell Collection*, W. & R. Chambers Ltd, Edinburgh, 1991. Accessible introduction to the stained glass in the Burrell Collection.

Marie Groll, *Thomas and Drake and the Transatlantic Trade in Stained Glass 1900–1950*. PhD thesis, University of York, 2016. Includes a major study on Drake's relationship with Burrell alongside their transcribed correspondence.

Richard Marks, *Stained Glass in England During the Middle Ages*, Routledge, London, 1993. An authoritative history of English medieval stained glass, with examples from the Burrell Collection.

Virginia Chieffo Raguin, *Stained Glass: From its Origins to the Present*, Harry N. Abrams, Inc., New York, 2003. Lavishly illustrated and thorough survey of stained glass from the ancient world to the present day.

Virginia Chieffo Raguin, *Stained Glass: Radiant Art*, The J. Paul Getty Museum, Los Angeles, 2013. Insightful pocket-sized introduction to medieval and Renaissance stained glass, illustrated with examples from the J. Paul Getty Museum.

Glossary

Abrasion – the process of grinding or scraping FLASHED GLASS, to reveal the white/clear glass beneath.

Calme/Came – an H-sectioned strip of lead that holds the glass pieces together.

Cartoon – a full-scale drawing of the window design, indicating details such as painted lines, glass colour, and the placement of lead CALMES.

Clerestory – the upper glazed storey of a church.

Enamels – colourants made from powdered coloured glass suspended in a liquid medium. Applied directly to glass like paint, then fused to the surface with firing.

Flashed glass – white or colourless glass coated with a thin layer of coloured glass. The coloured layer can be ground away with ABRASION.

Grisailles – panels of largely uncoloured glass, intricately leaded or painted with decorative ornamental designs. Sometimes finished with SILVER STAIN, and/or small amounts of coloured POT METAL glass.

Grozing – a means of shaping and trimming cut glass with a notched tool called a grozing iron, resulting in a distinctive nibbled edge.

Insertion – the process in which glass is abraded through, creating a hole which is filled with inserted glass.

Lancet window – a tall slender window terminating in a pointed arch.

Lights – a single window opening. Multiple lights divided by stone MULLIONS make up large Gothic windows.

Mullions – the vertical stone shafts that divide windows into individual LIGHTS.

Pot-metal – glass coloured throughout by the addition of metallic oxides introduced while in its molten state.

Silver stain – a means of staining white/clear glass yellow or orange, and blue glass green, by the application of a compound of silver. Usually applied to the outer surface of the glass, the colour becomes evident when fired. Also known as 'yellow stain'.

Tracery lights – small openings at the top of the main window.

Vitreous paint – a black-brown mixture of ground glass, metal oxides, and a binder such as wine, vinegar or urine, used to paint detail onto glass and fused to the surface when fired.